FELTED CROCHET

FELTED CROCHET

SIXTH&SPRING BOOKS
NEW YORK

SIXTH&SPRING BOOKS
233 Spring Street
New York, New York 10013

Library of Congress Cataloging-in-Publication Data
Library of Congress Control Number: 2007937709

ISBN-10: 1-933027-40-1
ISBN-13: 978-1-933027-40-1

Manufactured in China

1 3 5 7 9 10 8 6 4 2

First Edition, 2008

TABLE OF CONTENTS

INTRODUCTION

Look no further: Two of the hottest trends in fiber arts—felting and crochet—have joined forces. And the results, as you will see, are truly delightful!

Inside you will find felted variations of classic crochet motifs (see the lovely granny squares in the Baby Blanket on p. 80 and the Felted Rug on p. 35) as well as innovations combining form and function (check out the cute embellishments on the Structured Basket on p. 76). The dense texture of felting makes it a great candidate for projects that stand up, figuratively and often literally, to daily wear and tear (see the Striped Tote on p. 38 and the and Cell Phone Cozy on p. 22). And felted projects make perfect toys, withstanding years of love and mischief—the Penguin Toy on p. 42 can be hugged and squeezed for years without losing its cool, and the Race Car Toy on p. 28 will never collapse or unravel under the strain of kids' roughhousing.

Those of you just learning to crochet will love the instant gratification you get from small, simple projects. For a quick fix, check out the Rosette Scarf on p. 47 and the Camera Holder on p. 66. If you've already earned your stripes, so to speak, you will enjoy the rich colors and subtle shaping of the Southwestern Bag on p. 90.

Whether you are just starting out or are already crochet- or felting-obsessed, you will find plenty of projects to fuel your fire in these pages. So grab a hook, curl up and get ready to crochet **ON THE GO!**

THE BASICS

Felting is so easy, it can happen even when you don't want it to—as you already know if you've ever absentmindedly tossed a wool sweater in the washer and your beautiful cardigan comes out just the right size to fit your toddler. Heat, water and agitation cause the scales of the fiber to open up. As the fibers move past each other during agitation, the scales catch and stick together. The fibers become locked and your soft, flexible hand-knitting turns into a dense, matted fabric. Felting is permanent; once the wool fibers mesh together, there is no way to separate them. Called "felt" or "boiled wool," the resulting fabric is amazingly durable.

When knitting or crochet felts accidentally, it is a disaster. But when you felt intentionally, you can create beautiful pieces with unusual textures that will stand up to the roughest handling, and that will not unravel even when cut in pieces. Felting also hides flaws, so even beginning stitchers can have fun with this technique. Just sew up any misshapen or missed stitches, and they will disappear in the washing machine.

Traditionally, the term "felting" refers to the technique of using wool fleece to create felt, while "fulling" refers to the technique of using knitted or woven pieces. Today, the word felting is commonly used for both techniques.

Felted projects allow you to be creative, but not all yarns can be used for felting. Only yarns made from natural animal fibers will felt. One-hundred percent wool, mohair, cashmere, llama and alpaca are all excellent choices. (If you're a hand-spinner, dog hair also felts nicely.) If you choose a blend, make sure it contains at least 80% wool or mohair.

Most bleached white wools do not felt, although some manufacturers do have white yarn that felts. Felt a test swatch to check. Pastel colors and heathers are sometimes also slow to felt because the wool is often bleached before it is dyed. Superwash, or machine-washable, wool yarn has been treated by the manufacturer to prevent felting. Acrylic, cotton and plant fibers in general will not felt.

YARN SELECTION

Each item in this book has been crocheted and felted with the yarn listed in the MATERIALS section of the pattern. For best results use the recommended yarn in the colors as shown. We've selected yarns

GAUGE

It is always important to crochet a gauge swatch. In order to achieve the correct finished measurements after felting, it is imperative to get the gauge before felting. Therefore we have only given the gauge before felting. If you crochet to the suggested gauge, and felt according to the instructions, your project will turn out as intended.

Patterns usually state gauge over a 4"/10cm span; however, it's beneficial to make a larger test swatch. This gives a more precise stitch gauge, a better idea of the appearance and gives you a chance to familiarize yourself with the stitch pattern.

Measure gauge as illustrated. Try different needle sizes until your sample

measures the required number of stitches and rows. To get fewer stitches to the inch/cm, use a larger hook; to get more stitches to the inch/cm, use smaller hook.

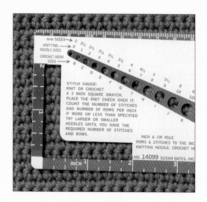

that are readily available in the U.S. and Canada at the time of printing. The Resources list on page 86 provides the addresses of the yarn distributors. Contact

them for the name of a retailer in your area.

Crochet is accessible and really quite easy to learn. Stitches are formed by pulling loops through other loops, or

CROCHET HOOKS					
U.S.	**Metric**	**U.S.**	**Metric**	**U.S.**	**Metric**
B/1	2.25mm	G/6	4mm	K/10.5	6.5mm
C/2	2.75mm	7	4.5mm	L/11	8mm
D/3	3.25mm	H/8	5mm	M/13	9mm
E/4	3.5mm	I/9	5.5mm	N/15	10mm
F/5	3.75mm	J/10	6mm		

stitches, with a hook, creating the simple chain that is used in all patterns. Unlike knitting, it requires no balancing act with needles, shifting stitches from one needle to another. In crochet, one hand and one hook do all the work, and finished fabric lies away from the hook, letting crocheters concentrate only on the next stitch they need to make. And, unlike other crafts, correcting a mistake is fairly stress-free— simply tug on the yarn to easily pull out the stitches you have worked.

If you're not convinced that it's easy to learn to crochet, perhaps the pieces in this collection will inspire you. They run the gamut from basic to more complicated stitches, giving experienced crocheters ample challenge and offering novices the chance to graduate to more difficult projects as they progress. The beginner styles, such as the Striped Tote on page 38 and the Rosette Scarf on page 47, often work up quickly. Such basic patterns let the yarn take center stage. Meanwhile, the more advanced designs, like the Southwestern Bag on page 90, do not necessarily have more difficult stitch techniques; rather, the instructions, with their series of repeats and pattern layouts, require more concentration to create the perfect piece.

READING CROCHET INSTRUCTIONS

If you are used to reading knitting instructions, then crochet instructions may seem a little tedious to follow. Crochet instructions use more abbreviations and punctuation and fewer words than traditional knitting instructions. Along with the separation of stitches and use of brackets, parentheses, commas and other punctuation, numerous repetitions may occur within a single row or round. Therefore, you must pay close attention to reading instructions while you crochet. Here are a few explanations of the more common terms used in this book.

Use of Parentheses ( )

Sometimes parentheses are used to indicate stitches that are to be worked all into one stitch, such as "in next st work ( )" or "( ) in next st."

First st, Next st

The beginning stitch of every row is referred to as the "first st." When counting the turning chain (t-ch) as 1 stitch, the row or round will begin by instructing that you work into the next st (that is, skip the first st or space or whatever is designated in the pattern).

Stitch Counts

Sometimes the turning chain that is worked at the end (or beginning) of a row or a round will be referred to as 1 stitch and is then counted in the stitch count. In those cases, you will work into the next stitch, thus skipping the first stitch of the

Categories of yarn, gauge ranges, and recommended needle and hook sizes

Yarn Weight Symbol & Category Names	Super Fine	Fine	Light	Medium	Bulky	Super Bulky
Type of Yarns in Category	Sock, Fingering, Baby	Sport, Baby	DK, Light Worsted	Worsted, Afghan, Aran	Chunky, Craft, Rug	Bulky, Roving
Knit Gauge Range* in Stockinette Stitch to 4 Inches	27–32 sts	23–26 sts	21–24 sts	16–20 sts	12–15 sts	6–11 sts
Recommended Needle in Metric Size Range	2.25–3.25 mm	3.25–3.75 mm	3.75–4.5 mm	4.5–5.5 mm	5.5–8 mm	8 mm and larger
Recommended Needle U.S. Size Range	1 to 3	3 to 5	5 to 7	7 to 9	9 to 11	11 and larger
Crochet Gauge* Ranges in Single Crochet To 4 Inches	21–32 sts	16–20 sts	12–17 sts	11–14 sts	8–11 sts	5–9 sts
Recommended Hook in Metric Size Range	2.25–3.5 mm	3.5–4.5 mm	4.5–5.5 mm	5.5–6.5 mm	6.5–9 mm	9 mm and larger
Recommended Hook U.S. Size Range	B–1 to E–4	E–4 to 7	7 to I–9	I–9 to K–10½	K–10½ to M–13	M–13 and larger

*Guidelines only: The above reflects the most commonly used needle or hook sizes for specific yarn categories.

■□□□

Beginner

Ideal first project.

■■□□

Very Easy

Basic stitches, minimal shaping, simple finishing.

Intermediate

For crocheters with some experience. More intricate stitches, shaping and finishing.

Experienced

For crocheters able to work patterns with complicated shaping and finishing.

row or round. When the turning chain is not counted as a stitch, work into the first actual stitch.

Stitches Described

Sometimes the stitches are described as sc, dc, tr, ch-2 loop, 2-dc group, etc., and sometimes—such as in a mesh pattern of sc, ch 1—each sc and each ch 1 will be referred to as a st.

Back Loop

Along the top of each crochet stitch or chain there are two loops. The loop furthest away from you is the "back loop."

Front Loop

Along the top of each crochet stitch or chain there are two loops. The loop closest to you is the "front loop."

Joining New Colors

When joining new colors in crochet, whether at the beginning of a row or while working across, always work the stitch in the old color to the last 2 loops, then draw the new color through the 2 loops and continue with the new color.

Working Over Ends

Crochet has a unique flat top along each row that is perfect for laying the old color across and working over the ends for several stitches. This will alleviate the need to cut and weave in ends later.

Form a Ring

When a pattern is worked in the round, as in a square or medallion, the beginning chains are usually closed into a ring by working a slip stitch into the first chain. Then on the first round, stitches are usually worked into the ring and less often into each chain.

BLOCKING

Blocking crochet is usually not necessary. However, in those cases when you do need to smooth out the fabric, choose a blocking method consistent with information on the yarn care label and, when in doubt, test your gauge swatch. Note that some yarns, such as chenilles and ribbons, do not benefit from blocking.

Wet Block Method

Using rustproof pins, pin scarf to measurements on a flat surface and lightly dampen using a spray bottle. Allow to dry before removing pins.

Steam Block Method

Pin scarf to measurements with wrong side of the fabric facing up. Steam lightly, holding the iron 2"/5cm above the work. Do not press the iron directly onto the piece, as it will flatten the stitches.

FELTING

Each pattern in this book has specific felting instructions as written by the designers. For best results, we recommend that you follow those directions when felting your knitted project. The following is an overview of basic techniques.

Felting by Machine

Machine felting can be done in top loaders and in newer front loaders that allow you to open the door during the wash cycle. If you have an older front loader that locks during the wash cycle, you will not be able to check the felting progress to control the amount of shrinkage.

Place the knitted item in a zippered pillow case or mesh bag to catch any stray lint. Put the bag in the washing machine with an old pair of jeans or an old towel for added agitation. (Make sure the pockets are empty—any lint that gets into the felt will be stuck forever.) Set the machine for the smallest load size with a hot wash, and add a small amount of soap. Close the lid and turn on the machine.

Check the progress every five minutes until the desired size is achieved. Reset the agitation cycle if necessary. Some yarns may felt in a few minutes, while others may take several cycles.

When the fibers are matted and you don't want the item to shrink any more, take it out and gently rinse it in tepid water in the sink. Roll the item in a towel and squeeze out the excess water. Do NOT wring—it may pull the item out of shape!

Felting by Hand

Felting by hand is more labor intensive than felting by machine, but it wastes less water, particularly when you are felting a swatch or a small project.

Soak the finished item in hot water for thirty minutes or until it is completely saturated. Add a small amount of soap. Agitate the piece by rubbing and kneading. This may take some time, so be patient. If the water cools, add more hot water.

When the fibers are matted and you don't want the item to shrink any more, rinse it in tepid water. Roll item in a towel and squeeze out excess water. Do NOT wring—it may pull the item out of shape!

BLOCKING AND FINISHING

After felting and rinsing your item, trim off any stray ends that popped out during felting. If the edge of a piece flares and you can't flatten it by pressing, baste it with thread and gather the edge until it is flat. Remove the basting thread when the piece is dry.

■ Block bags and hats using blocking forms, bowls, or plates.

■ Shape mittens with your hand, and slippers with your foot.

■ Small plastic bags work well for holding pieces in shape while drying. Once the felted item is shaped, gently stuff it with several crumpled bags.

■ Steam press garment pieces and home décor items and block to pattern measurements. Using rustproof pins, pin the piece on a flat surface and allow to dry before removing the pins.

If the felted texture is too furry, use a dog or cat brush to make the fur on the surface of the felt stand up. Then cut the fur off using very sharp sewing shears to reveal the smooth, dense felt underneath. Be careful not to cut into the actual knitting.

Refer to the yarn label for the recommended cleaning method. Many of the projects in the book can be either washed by hand, or in the machine using no-rinse wool-wash soap. Do not agitate and don't soak for more than 10 minutes. (Agitating felted items in the washing machine may cause them to shrink more.) Fold in a towel and gently press the water out. Block and leave to air dry away from direct sunlight. To speed up the drying process, place the item near a heating vent or on top of the clothes dryer while it is use.

Felting is an art, not a science. You may use the exact yarn specified in a project and follow the directions precisely, and still be surprised with the results of felting. Many times these "mistakes" can easily be fixed.

■ Too small: While the item is wet, stretch it.

■ Too big: Run the item through additional agitation cycles in the washing machine.

■ Too long: Cut bags or garment pieces to shorten. Embellish the cut edge with crochet or embroidery if desired.

■ Colors felt differently: Use hand felting

to shrink the larger areas until they match the smaller areas.

■ Colors run: Carefully use Rit® Color Remover to clean the affected areas.

Although it is best to use the recommended yarns in the colors as shown in this book, you may choose to substitute the yarns. Perhaps a spectacular yarn matches your favorite coat or an antique chair in your living room; maybe you view small-scale projects as a chance to incorporate leftovers from your yarn stash; or perhaps the yarn specified is not available in your area.

Some projects use a strand of wool held together with a strand of novelty yarn. The wool felts, locking the novelty yarn into place and creating beautiful and unique textures. You can substitute for both yarns as long as at least one of the strands is a fiber that will felt. Be sure to consider how different yarn types (wool, mohair, eyelash, etc.) will affect the final appearance of your project and how it will feel against your skin if used for a garment.

For an item to felt properly, your gauge should be loose enough so that you can see space between the stitches. If stitches are too tight, your piece may take a long time to felt and, even after a long period of agitation, may not shrink enough. Always crochet and felt a gauge swatch before making a final decision about yarn substitution. After you've successfully crocheted and felted the swatch with substitute yarn, you'll need to figure out how much of the substitute yarn the project requires. First, find the total length of the original yarn in the pattern (multiply the number of balls by yards/meters per ball). Divide this figure by the new yards/meters per ball (listed on the ball band). Round up to the next whole number. The answer is the number of balls required, but be sure to purchase extra yarn for swatching. Remember, once yarn has been felted, it cannot be reused.

To make a swatch for felting, chain 30 sts and crochet in the pattern stitch used in your project for 40 rows. Both before and after you felt your swatch, measure its length and width.

■ Divide the width by 30 (number of stitches). This gives number of stitches per inch.

■ Divide the length by 40. This gives the number of rows per inch.

You may not be able to see the stitches after the swatch is felted. This process allows you to measure the gauge after felting without being able to count stitches or rows.

Compare your felted test swatch to the finished measurements in the pattern to see if the yarn is suitable for the pattern.

If you plan to make a large item, always knit and felt a large test swatch. A small swatch will not give accurate results. However for a small item, work a small swatch. When substituting or trying a new pattern with expensive yarns, it is a good idea to test the shrinkage.

When substituting yarns—whether combining different yarns in one project or using different colors of the same yarn—felting a swatch is critical. The yarns or colors you have chosen may not felt at the same rate, or the colors may bleed onto each other.

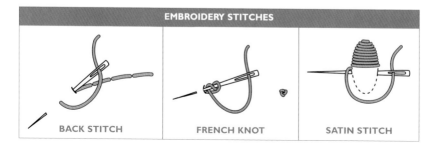

EMBROIDERY STITCHES

BACK STITCH   FRENCH KNOT   SATIN STITCH

CHAIN

I *Pass the yarn over the hook and catch it with the hook.*

2 *Draw the yarn through the loop on the hook.*

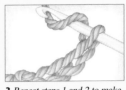

3 *Repeat steps 1 and 2 to make a chain.*

SINGLE CROCHET

I *Insert the hook through top two loops of a stitch. Pass the yarn over the hook and draw up a loop—two loops on hook.*

2 *Pass the yarn over the hook and draw through both loops on hook.*

3 *Continue in the same way, inserting the hook into each stitch.*

HALF-DOUBLE CROCHET

I *Pass the yarn over the hook. Insert the hook through the top two loops of a stitch.*

2 *Pass the yarn over the hook and draw up a loop—three loops on hook. Pass the yarn over the hook.*

3 *Draw through all three loops on hook.*

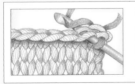

DOUBLE CROCHET

I *Pass the yarn over the hook. Insert the hook through the top two loops of a stitch.*

2 *Pass the yarn over the hook and draw up a loop—three loops on hook.*

SLIP STITCH

Insert the crochet hook into a stitch, catch the yarn and pull up a loop. Draw the loop through the loop on the hook.

3 *Pass the yarn over the hook and draw it through the first two loops on the hook, pass the yarn over the hook and draw through the remaining two loops. Continue in the same way, inserting the hook into each stitch.*

Illustrations: Joni Coniglio

CROCHET TERMS AND ABBREVIATIONS

approx approximately

beg begin(ning)

CC contrast color

ch chain(s)

cm centimeter(s)

cont continue(ing)

dc double crochet (U.K.: tr-treble)

dec decrease(ing)–Reduce the stitches in a row (work stitches together or skip the stitches).

foll follow(s)(ing)

g gram(s)

hdc half double crochet (U.K.: htr-half treble)

inc increase(ing)–Add stitches in a row (work extra stitches into a stitch or between the stitches).

LH left-hand

lp(s) loop(s)

m meter(s)

MC main color

mm millimeter(s)

oz ounce(s)

pat(s) pattern

pm place markers–Place or attach a loop of contrast yarn or purchased stitch marker as indicated.

rem remain(s)(ing)

rep repeat

rnd(s) round(s)

RH right-hand

RS right side(s)

sc single crochet (U.K.: dc-double crochet)

sk skip

sl st slip stitch (U.K.: single crochet)

sp(s) space(s)

st(s) stitch(es)

t-ch turning chain

tog together

tr treble (U.K.: tr tr-triple treble)

WS wrong side(s)

work even Continue in pattern without increasing or decreasing. (U.K.: work straight)

yd yard(s)

yo yarn over–Wrap the yarn around the hook (U.K.: yrh)

* Repeat directions following * as many times as indicated.

[ ] Repeat directions inside brackets as many times as indicated.

SQUARE PURSE

Ocean Avenue

Crochet this trendy little daytime purse in just an evening. Chunky yarn makes it quick work, and the self–striping effect takes out all the fuss of finishing. Designed by Alexandra Lockhart.

FINISHED MEASUREMENTS
■ Approx 11½"/29cm wide x 9½"/24cm high

MATERIALS
■ 4 1.75oz/50g balls (each approx 88yd/80m) of Nashua Handknits/Westminster Fibers, Inc. *Wooly Stripes* (wool) in #51 jungle greens (**4**)
■ Size K/10½ (6.5mm) crochet hook *or size to obtain gauge*
■ Seven safety pins (one a different color)

GAUGE
10 sts and 9 rnds to 4"/10cm over hdc using size K/10½ (6.5mm) crochet hook (before felting).
Take time to check gauge.

TOTE

Ch 36.

Rnd I (RS) Work 3 hdc in 2nd ch from hook (mark these 3 sts with safety pins to indicate corner), hdc in next 33 ch, work 3 hdc in last ch (mark these 3 sts with safety pins to indicate corner), turn to bottom lps of foundation ch, hdc in next 34 bottom lps—73 sts. Mark last st made with the different color safety pin. You will be working in a spiral marking the last st made with the different color safety pin to indicate end of rnd.

Rnd 2 [Work 2 hdc in next marked corner st] 3 times (dropping corner safety pins), hdc in each st to next 3 marked corner sts, [work 2 hdc in next marked corner st] 3 times (dropping corner safety pins), hdc in each st to end—79 sts.

Rnds 3–23 Hdc in each st around. Do not fasten off.

HANDLES

On front of purse, mark for handle opening as foll: locate center st, count 6 sts to the right of center st and mark the 6th st with a safety pin. Count 6 sts to the left of center st and mark 6th st with a safety pin. Rep on back of purse.

Rnd 24 [Hdc in each st to next marked st, ch 13, skip next 13 sts] twice, hdc in each st to end. Drop handle safety pins.

Rnd 25 Hdc in each st around, working 13 hdc over each ch–13 lp.

Rnds 26–29 Hdc in each st and ch around. Fasten off.

FINISHING

Felting

Place purse in a zippered pillowcase and put into washing machine. Use hot-water wash, a regular (not delicate) cycle and lowest water level. Add a tablespoon of laundry detergent and an old pair of jeans for agitation. Check piece frequently, agitating until stitches are not seen and purse measures 11½"/29cm wide x 9½"/24cm high. Rinse in cold water; do not allow to go through spin cycle. Remove from pillowcase, then gently roll in towels to assist in drying if purse is extremely wet. Stretch into shape. Let air dry flat.

CELL PHONE COZY

Ring-a-ding-ding

Keep your mobile phone safe from dings and scratches when you store it in this adorable little cozy. The handy flower-accented strap unsnaps in a wink for easy access. Designed by Linda Cyr.

FINISHED MEASUREMENTS

■ Approx 3"/7.5cm wide x 4½"/11.5cm high (excluding strap)

MATERIALS

■ 1 2oz/78g skein (each approx 143yd/131m) of Lion Brand Yarn *Lion Wool Prints* (wool) in #201 autumn sunset (MC) (4)

■ 1 3oz/85g skein (each approx 158yds/144m) of Lion Brand Yarn *Lion Wool* (wool) in #132 lemongrass (CC) (4)

■ Size H/8 (5mm) crochet hook *or size to obtain gauge*

■ One ⅜"/1cm metal snap set

■ Matching sewing thread

■ Sewing needle

■ Small safety pin

GAUGE

14 sts and 17 rnds to 4"/10cm over sc using size H/8 (5mm) crochet hook (before felting). *Take time to check gauge.*

STITCH GLOSSARY

sc2tog [Insert hook in next st, yo and draw up a lp] twice, yo and draw through all 3 lps on hook.

COZY

Beg at bottom edge, with MC, ch 18. Join ch with a sl st in first ch, taking care not to twist ch.

Rnd 1 (RS) Sc in each ch around. Mark last st made with the safety pin. You will be working in a spiral marking the last st made with the safety pin to indicate end of rnd.

Rnd 2 [Sc in next 2 sts, work 2 sc in next st] 6 times—24 sts.

Rnd 3 [Sc in next 3 sts, work 2 sc in next st] 6 times—30 sts.

Rnds 4–12 Sc in each st around.

Rnd 13 [Sc in next 3 sts, sc2tog] 6 times—24 sts.

Rnd 14 Sc in each st around. Do not fasten off.

Strap

Ch 30.

Row 1 Sc in 2nd ch from hook and in each ch across, then sc in edge of cozy—30 sts. Turn.

Row 2 Ch 1, sc in each st across. Turn.

Row 3 Ch 1, sc in each sc across, then sl st in each st around top edge of cozy, join with a sl st to side edge of strap. Fasten off.

FLOWER

With CC, ch 6.

Rnd 1 Sl st in 6th ch from hook, [ch 5, sl st in same ch as first sl st] 5 times—6 petals. Fasten off.

Whipstitch bottom edge of cozy closed.

Felting cozy

Place cozy in a zippered pillowcase and put into washing machine. Use hot-water wash, a regular (not delicate) cycle and the lowest water level. Add a tablespoon of laundry detergent and an old pair of jeans for agitation. Check piece frequently, agitating until stitches are not seen and cozy measures 3"/7.5cm wide x 4½"/11.5cm high. Rinse in cold water, then remove piece from pillowcase. Roll cozy in towels to remove most of the water. Dry in dryer until slightly damp. Block with your hands to measurements, then stuff lightly with a folded plastic grocery bag to hold its shape. Place on flat surface to dry, making sure strap is flat and straight. Allow to dry completely.

Felting flower

Place flower in a bowl of hot water. Add a drop of detergent, then gently agitate using a rubber spatula. Leave flower in water for 15 minutes, then rinse in cold water. Press out excess water using a terry towel. Shape flower, then allow to air dry. On WS of strap, position top half of snap so edge of snap is ¼"/.6cm from end of strap and is centered side to side. Sew snap in place using sewing thread. On RS of cozy, position bottom half of snap on side opposite strap, so edge of snap is ¼"/.6cm from top edge of cozy; sew in place. Sew flower to end of strap so petals extend beyond edge.

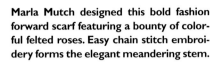

Marla Mutch designed this bold fashion forward scarf featuring a bounty of colorful felted roses. Easy chain stitch embroidery forms the elegant meandering stem.

FINISHED MEASUREMENTS
Scarf
■ Approx 7"/17.5cm wide x 88"/216cm long
Rose
■ Approx 3¾"/9.5cm wide
Large leaf
■ Approx 3¼"/8cm wide x 3¾"/9.5cm long
Small leaf
■ Approx 2½"/6cm wide x 3"/7.5cm long

MATERIALS
■ 2 3.5oz/100g balls (each approx 127yd/116m) of Classic Elite Yarns *Montera* (llama/wool) in #3813 black (MC) ■4■
■ 1 ball each in #3882 bold rose (A), #3853 black cherry (B) and #3840 tuscan hills (C)
■ Sizes I/9 and J/10 (5.5 and 6mm) crochet hooks *or size needed to obtain gauge*

GAUGE
9 sts and 14 rows to 4"/10cm over sc rib pat using smaller crochet hook.
Take time to check gauge.
Notes
1 Only the roses and leaves are felted.
2 To join yarn with a sc, make a slip knot and place on hook. Insert hook into st, yo and draw up a lp, yo and draw through both lps on hook.

STITCH GLOSSARY
sc2tog [Insert hook in next st, yo and draw up a lp] twice, yo and draw through all 3 lps on hook.
sc3tog [Insert hook in next st, yo and draw up a lp] 3 times, yo and draw through all 4 lps on hook.

SCARF
With smaller hook and MC, ch 151.
Row 1 Sc in 2nd ch from hook and in each ch across—150 sts. Turn.
Row 2 Ch 1, working in back lps only, sc in each st across. Turn. Rep row 2 for sc rib pat until piece measures 7"/17.5cm from beg. Change to larger hook. Turn to short side edge of scarf.
Ruffle edging
Row 1 (RS) Ch 1, sc in side edge of first row, [ch 7, skip 1"/2.5cm, sc in side edge of next row] 7 times. Turn.
Row 2 Ch 1, sc in first sc, [work (sc, 6 dc, sc) in next ch-7 lp, sc in next sc] 7 times. Fasten off. With larger hook and RS of opposite short side edge facing, join MC with a sc in side edge of first row.
Row 1 (RS) [Ch 7, skip 1"/2.5cm, sc in side edge of next row] 7 times. Turn.
Rep row 2 as for first short side edge. Fasten off.

ROSES (MAKE 6)
With larger hook and A, ch 6. Join ch with a sl st forming a ring.
First row of petals
Rnd 1 (RS) [Ch 6, sc in ring] 6 times—6 petal bases.
Rnd 2 [Work (sc, 6 dc, sc) in next ch-6 lp] 6 times—6 petals. Fasten off.

Second row of petals

With RS facing and working between 2 sc of rnd 1, join A with a sc in ring.

Rnd 1 (RS) [Ch 6, sc in ring between next 2 sc of rnd 1] 6 times—6 petal bases.

Rnd 2 Rep rnd 2. Fasten off.

Third row of petals

With RS facing and working between pairs of sc of rnd 1, join A with a sc in ring.

Rnd 1 (RS) [Ch 6, sc in ring between pairs of sc of rnd 1] 6 times—6 petal bases.

Rnd 2 Rep rnd 2. Fasten off.

Make 2 more roses using A and 3 more using B.

With smaller hook and C, ch 2.

Note You will not ch after turning, so edges will curl in, forming a cupped, shaped leaf.

Row 1 (RS) Work 3 sc in 2nd ch from hook—3 sts. Turn.

Row 2 Work 2 sc in first st, sc in next st, work 2 sc in last st—5 sts. Turn.

Row 3 Work 2 sc in first st, sc in each st to last st, work 2 sc in last st—7 sts. Turn.

Rows 4–7 Rep row 3—15 sts. Turn.

Row 8 Sc2tog, sc in each st to last 2 sts, sc2tog—13 sts. Turn.

Rows 9–14 Rep row 8—3 sts. Turn.

Row 15 Sc3tog. Fasten off.

With smaller hook and C, ch 2.

Note You will not ch after turning, so edges will curl in, forming a cupped, shaped leaf.

Row 1 (RS) Work 3 sc in 2nd ch from hook—3 sts. Turn.

Row 2 Work 2 sc in first st, sc in next st, work 2 sc in last st—5 sts. Turn.

Row 3 Work 2 sc in first st, sc in each st to last st, work 2 sc in last st—7 sts. Turn.

Rows 4 and 5 Rep row 3—11 sts. Turn.

Row 6 Sc2tog, sc in each st to last 2 sts, sc2tog—9 sts. Turn.

Rows 7–9 Rep row 6—3 sts. Turn.

Row 10 Sc3tog. Fasten off.

Using C, sew a large leaf and a small leaf to bottom of each rose.

Felting

Place assembled roses in a zippered pillowcase and put into washing machine. Use hot-water wash and a regular (not delicate) cycle. Add a tablespoon of laundry detergent and an old pair of jeans for agitation. Check pieces frequently, agitating until stitches are not seen and roses measure 3¾"/9.5cm. Rinse in cold water and remove pieces from pillowcase. Shape roses and leaves to finished measurements, then allow to air dry for 1 to 2 days.

Embroidery

Working in chain stitch and using C, embroider a meandering rose stem along the entire length of the scarf. Sew 2 A roses and 1 B rose evenly spaced on one end of scarf, then 2 B roses and 1 A rose evenly spaced on opposite end.

■■■▢

Racers, start your engines! Your little tot's imagination will take off for lots of fast-paced playtime fun with this sleek race car and pit crew trio. The mag wheels are attached with Velcro® tabs so they can come off and on in no time flat. Designed by PD Cagliastro.

Race car

■ Approx 6½"/16.5cm wide x 13½"/34cm long x 6"/15cm tall (excluding wheels)

Pit crew

■ Approx 11½"/29cm tall

■ 2 3.5oz/100g skeins (each approx 223yd/205m) of Patons *Classic Merino Wool* (wool) each in #77134 that's blue, #77707 that's red, #226 black and #201 winter white (**4**)

■ Size H/8 (5mm) crochet hook

■ 6"/16cm of ⅞"/22mm wide black Velcro

■ Sewing needle and threads to match

■ Polyester fiberfill

■ Small safety pin

Gauge is not important.

Notes

1 Use 2 strands of yarn held tog throughout.
2 To join yarn with a sc, make a slip knot and place on hook. Insert hook into st (or row), yo and draw up a lp, yo and draw through both lps on hook.

3 When changing colors, draw new color through last 2 lps on hook when working last st.

sc2tog [Insert hook in next st, yo and draw up a lp] twice, yo and draw through all 3 lps on hook.

Hood

With 2 strands of blue held tog, ch 26.

Row 1 (RS) Sc in 2nd ch from hook and in each ch across—25 sts. Turn.

Rows 2–20 Ch 1, sc in each st across. Turn.

Upper side panels (b head)

Row 21 Ch 1, sc in first 6 sts leaving rem sts unworked. Turn.

Rows 22–36 Ch 1, sc in each st across. Fasten off. With RS facing, skip center 13 sts (bottom edge of front windshield), join 2 strands of blue with a sc in next st, sc in last 5 sts. Turn. Rep rows 22–36. Fasten off.

Back end

Join blue yarn to end of row 36 of 1st side panel.

Row 37 (RS) Ch 1, sc in first 6 sts, ch 13, sc in 6 sts from opposite top side. Turn.

Rows 38 and 39 Ch 6, sc in 2nd ch from hook and in each st and ch across—35 sts. Turn.

Rows 40–51 Ch 1, sc2tog, sc in each st to last 2 sts, sc2tog—11 sts. Turn. When row 51 is completed, do not turn; fasten off.

Front windshield, roof and rear windshield

Row 1 (RS) With RS facing, join 2 strands of red in first skipped st of bottom edge of front windshield, sc in next 12 sts that were skipped—13 sts. Turn.

Rows 2–23 Ch 1, sc in each st across. Turn.

Row 24 Ch 1, sc in each st across changing to 2 strands of black. Turn.

Row 25 Rep row 2.

Rows 26–29 Ch 1, sc2tog, sc in each st to last 2 sts, sc2tog—9 sts. Fasten off leaving a long tail for sewing. Overlap rear windshield on upper section of trunk and whipstitch in place using tail. This forms openings for driver's side and passenger's side windows.

Passenger side window

Position upper body of car so roof is at top and rear end is at your left.

Row 1 (RS) With RS facing, join 2 strands of black with a sc in right side edge of window opening, work 16 sc more evenly spaced across opening.

Rows 2–6 Ch 1, sc2tog, sc in each st to last 2 sts, sc2tog—7 sts. Turn. When row 6 is completed, do not turn; fasten off leaving a long tail for sewing. Whipstitch window to opening using tail.

Driver side window

Position upper body of car so roof is at top and rear end is at your right. Cont to work As for passenger side window.

SIDE PANELS (MAKE 2 PIECES)

Beg at front end, with 2 strands of red held tog, ch 11.

Row 1 Sc in 2nd ch from hook and in each ch across—10 sts. Turn.

Rows 2 and 3 Ch 1, sc in each st across. Turn.

Row 4 Ch 1, sc2tog, sc in each rem st across—9 sts. Turn.

Row 5 Rep row 2.

Row 6 Rep row 4—8 sts.

Rows 7–37 Rep row 2.

Row 38 Ch 1, work 2 sc in first st, sc in each rem st across—9 sts. Turn.

Row 39 Ch 1, sc in each st to last st, work 2 sc in last st—10 sts. Turn.

Row 40 Rep row 38—11 sts.

Row 41 Ch 1, sc2tog, sc in each st to last 2 sts, sc2tog—9 sts. Turn.

Rows 42 and 43 Rep row 41—5 sts.

Row 44 Ch 1, work 2 sc in first st, sc in each st to last st, work 2 sc in last st—7 sts. Turn.

Rows 45 Ch 1, work 2 sc in first st, sc in each rem st across—8 sts. Turn.

Rows 46 and 47 Ch 1, sc in each st across. Turn.

Row 48 Ch 1, sc in each st to last 2 sts, sc2tog—7 sts. Turn.

Row 49 Ch 1, sc2tog, sc in each rem st across—6 sts. Turn.

Rows 50–53 Rep rows 48 and 49—2 sts.

Rows 54–60 Rep row 46. Fasten off leaving a long tail for sewing.

Beg at front end, with 2 strands of white held tog, ch 26.

Row 1 (RS) Sc in 2nd ch from hook and in each ch across—25 sts. Turn.

Rows 2–12 Ch 1, sc in each st across. Turn. When row 12 is completed, mark beg and end of last row for beg of underbody.

Underbody

Row 13 Ch 1, sc in each ch across—25 sts. Turn.

Rows 14–49 Ch 1, sc in each st across. Turn.

Rows 50 and 51 Ch 6, sc in 2nd ch from hook and in each st and ch across—35 sts. Turn.

Rows 52–55 Ch 1, sc in each st across. Turn.

Rows 56–67 Ch 1, sc2tog, sc in each st to last 2 sts, sc2tog—11 sts. Turn. When row 67 is completed, do not turn; fasten off.

Front

With 2 strands of blue held tog, ch 3. Join ch with a sl st forming a ring.

Rnd 1 (RS) Work 6 sc in ring. Mark last st made with the safety pin. You will be working in a spiral marking the last st made with the safety pin to indicate end of rnd.

Rnd 2 Work 2 sc in each sc around—12 sts.

Rnd 3 [Sc in next st, work 2 sc in next st] 6 times changing to 2 strands of black—18 sts.

Rnd 4 [Sc in next 2 sts, work 2 sc in next st] 6 times—24 sts.

Rnd 5 [Sc in next 3 sts, work 2 sc in next st] 6 times—30 sts.

Rnd 6 [Sc in next 4 sts, work 2 sc in next st] 6 times changing to 2 strands of white—36 sts.

Rnd 7 [Sc in next 5 sts, work 2 sc in next st] 6 times changing to 2 strands of black—42 sts.

Rnd 8 Sc in each st around. Fasten off leaving a long tail for sewing.

Back

With 2 strands of black held tog, ch 3. Join ch with a sl st forming a ring. Work rnds 1–7. As for front using black only. Make 3 more wheels using the same color sequence. For 2 spare wheels, use red for first 3 rnds of front.

Sew last row of each lower side panel together. Centering this seam at center of back end, pin top edge of lower side panels to bottom edge of upper side panels and back end of car. Using 2 strands of black, whipstitch pieces together.

Racing stripe (make 2 pieces)

With 2 strands of red held tog, ch 24.

Row 1 (RS) Sc in 2nd ch from hook and in each ch across. Turn.

Row 2 Sc in each st across. Fasten off leaving a long tail for sewing. Pin each stripe down hood as shown. Whipstitch striped in place using tails.

Trunk medallion

Work rnds 1–6 as for front wheel using 2 strands of white held tog. Fasten off leaving a long tail for sewing.

Side door medallion (make 2 pieces)

Work rnds 1–3 as for front wheel using 2 strands of white held tog. Fasten off leaving a long tail for sewing.

Embroidery

Use 2 strands of red, embroider a backstitch number 7 on center of trunk medallion and side door medallions. Use tails to whipstitch medallions to car. Using 2 strands of black, whipstitch bottom edge of front end to front edge of hood. Using 2 strands of red, whipstitch underbody to bottom edge of car, leaving a 4"/10cm opening. Stuff with fiberfill; whipstitch opening closed.

Wheels

Whipstitch a front to a back, leaving a 2"/5cm opening. Stuff with fiberfill; whipstitch opening closed.

Felting race car and wheels

Place race car in one zippered pillowcase and wheels in another zippered pillowcase. Place in washing machine. Use hot-water wash, a regular (not delicate) cycle and lowest water level. Add ¼ cup of laundry detergent and an old pair of jeans for agitation. Check pieces every 5–10 minutes, agitating until stitches are not seen and race car measures 6½"/16.5cm wide x 15½"/39.5cm long x 6"/15cm tall, and wheels measure 3¾"/9.5cm in diameter. Rinse in cold water and remove from pillowcases. Machine–dry for 10 minutes. Hand-block to measurements. Let air dry flat for 1 to 3 days. Cut 6 ⅞"/22mm lengths of Velcro. Sew one furry side of Velcro to race car for each wheel. Sew one hook side to center back of each wheel. Discard rem furry sides of Velcro.

Shoes

With 2 strands of blue held tog, ch 3. Join ch with a sl st forming a ring.

Rnd 1 (RS) Work 6 sc in ring. Mark last st made with the safety pin. You will be working in a spiral marking the last st made with the safety pin to indicate end of rnd.

Rnd 2 Work 2 sc in each st around—12 sts.

Rnd 3 [Sc in next st, work 2 sc in next st] 6 times—18 sts.

Rnd 4 [Sc in next 2 sts, work 2 sc in next st] 6 times—24 sts.

Rnd 5 [Sc in next 3 sts, work 2 sc in next st] 6 times—30 sts.

Rnd 6 [Sc in next 4 sts, work 2 sc in next st] 6 times—36 sts.

Rnd 7 [Sc in next 5 sts, work 2 sc in next st] 6 times changing to 2 strands of red—42 sts.

Pants

Rnd 8 [Sc in next 6 sts, work 2 sc in next st] 6 times—48 sts.

Rnds 9–17 Sc in each st around.

Rnd 18 [Sc in next 6 sts, sc2tog] 6 times—42 sts.

Rnd 19 [Sc in next 5 sts, sc2tog] 6 times—36 sts.

Rnd 20 Sc in each st around, changing to 2 strands of black.

Belt

Row 21 Sc in each st around.

Rnd 22 [Sc in next 4 sts, sc2tog] 6 times, changing to 2 strands of blue—30 sts.

Shirt

Rnds 23–28 Sc in each st around.

Rnd 29 Sc in each st around changing to 2 strands of white.

Head

Rnds 30 and 31 Sc in each st around.

Rnd 32 [Sc in next 4 sts, work 2 sc in next st] 6 times—36 sts.

Rnds 33–37 Sc in each st around.

Rnd 38 [Sc in next 5 sts, work 2 sc in next st] 6 times, changing to 2 strands of red—42 sts.

Cap

Rnds 39 and 40 Sc in each st around. Stuff body with fiberfill.

Rnd 41 [Sc in next 5 sts, sc2tog] 6 times—36 sts.

Rnd 42 [Sc in next 4 sts, sc2tog] 6 times—30 sts.

Rnd 43 [Sc in next 3 sts, sc2tog] 6 times—24 sts.

Rnd 44 [Sc in next 2 sts, sc2tog] 6 times—18 sts.

Rnd 45 [Sc in next st, sc2tog] 6 times—12 sts.

Rnd 46 [Sc2tog] 6 times—6 sts. Fasten off leaving a long tail for sewing. Stuff head with fiberfill. Sew top opening closed.

Brim

With 2 strands of black held tog, ch 14.

Row 1 (RS) Sc in 2nd ch from hook and in each ch across—13 sts. Turn.

Rows 2–5 Ch 1, sc2tog, sc in each st to last 2 sts, sc2tog. Turn. When row 5 is completed, do not turn; fasten off 5 sts.

Edging

With RS facing, join 2 strands of red with a sc in side edge of first row.

Row 1 (RS) Sc evenly along curved edge of brim. Fasten off leaving a long tail for sewing.

Arm (make 2 pieces)

With 2 strands of red held tog, ch 14.

Row 1 Sc in 2nd ch from hook and in each ch across—13 sts. Turn.

Row 2 Sl st in first 3 sts, sc in last 10 sts. Turn.

Row 3 Sc in first 7 sts, sl st in next st. Fasten off.

Hand

With side edge of 3 complete rows facing, join 2 strands of red with a sl st in side edge of first row.

Row 1 Ch 3 (counts as 1 dc), work 1 dc in side edge of first row, 1 dc in side of 2nd row, then 2 dc in side edge of 3rd row. Fasten off.

Work as for pit crew person 1, using red for shoes, blue for pants, black for belt, red for shirt, white for head and blue for cap. Use red for brim, then use blue for edging. Use blue for arms and hands.

Work as for pit crew person 1, using white for shoes, black for pants, red for belt, blue for shirt, white for head and black for cap. Use blue for brim, then use black for edging. Use black for arms and hands.

Position doll so color changes are at center back. Whipstitch cap brim to center front of head between rnds 38 and 39 using tails. Sew arms to each side of body.

Embroidery

Use 2 strands of yarn held tog throughout. Embroider horizontal satin stitch eyes using black, then a straight stitch mouth using red. Using same color as shirt, embroider a straight stitch number 7 on center front of cap.

Felting pit crew

Place each doll in a separate zippered pillowcase. Cont to felt as for race car, until each doll measures 11½"/29cm tall. Wheels will adhere to doll by simply pressing in place.

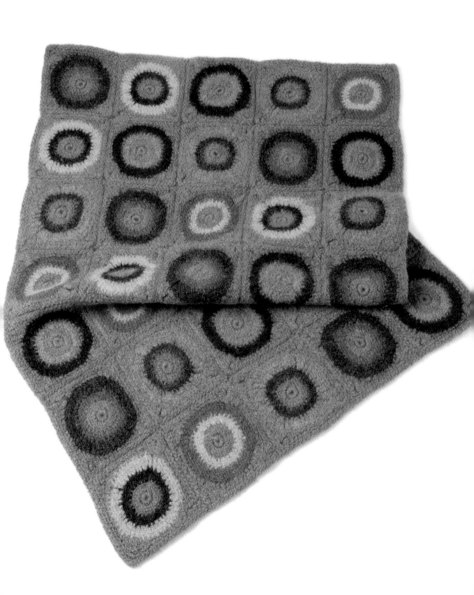

A hand-hooked rug can take a long time to make (or a ton of money to buy). You can get the same look in no time flat when you felt stitched–together crocheted squares. Simona Merchant–Dest designed it in a palette of colors that capture the spirit of Colonial America.

FINISHED MEASUREMENTS
■ Approx 24" x 34½"/61 x 87.5cm

MATERIALS
■ 4 3.5oz/100g hanks (each approx 174yd/160m) of Berroco, Inc, *Peruvia* (Peruvian highland wool) in color #7122 avocado (MC) (■4)
■ 1 hank each in #7120 maiz (A), #7132 tomate (B), #7110 naranja (C), #7108 tabaco (D) and #7125 sea turtle (E)
■ Size H/8 (5mm) crochet hook *or size to obtain gauge*

GAUGE
One square to 6"/15cm using size H/8 (5mm) crochet hook (before felting).
Take time to check gauge.

SQUARE (MAKE 35)
Make 35 squares foll placement diagram for colorways. With MC color, ch 3. Join ch with a sl st forming a ring.

Rnd 1 (RS) Ch 1, work 12 sc in ring, join rnd with a sl st in first st.

Rnd 2 Ch 3 (counts as 1 dc), dc in same sp as joining, *work 2 dc in next st; rep from * around, join rnd with a sl st in top of beg ch-3—24 sts. Fasten off.

Rnd 3 With RS facing, join next color with a sl st in same sp as joining, ch 3 (counts as 1 dc), dc in same sp as joining, *dc in next st, work 2 dc in next st; rep from * around, end dc in last st, join rnd with a sl st in top of beg ch-3—36 sts. Fasten off.

Rnd 4 With RS facing, join next color with a sl st in same sp as joining, ch 4 (counts as 1 tr), tr in same sp as joining, *tr in next 2 sts, work 2 tr in next st; rep from * around, end tr in last 2 sts, join rnd with a sl st in top of beg ch-4—48 sts. Fasten off.

Rnd 5 With RS facing, join MC with a sl st in same sp as joining, ch 1, *sc in next 7 sts, hdc in next st, dc in next st, work (tr, dtr, ch 1, dtr, tr) in next st (corner made), dc in next st, hdc in next st; rep from * around, join rnd with a sl st in top of beg ch-1.

Rnd 6 Ch 1, *sc in next 10 sts, skip dtr, work (sc, dc, sc) in next corner ch-1 sp, skip dtr, sc in next 3 sts; rep from * around, join rnd with a sl st in first st. Fasten off.

FINISHING
Block squares to measurements. Using MC and working in back lps, whipstitch squares tog foll placement diagram.

Edging
With RS facing, join MC with sl st in any corner dc, ch 1, work (sc, dc, sc) in same sp, *sc in each st to next corner, work (sc, dc, sc) in corner dc; rep from * around twice

more, end sc in each st to end, join rnd with a sl st in first sc. Fasten off.

Felting

Place rug in a zippered pillowcase and put into washing machine. Use hot-water wash, a regular (not delicate) cycle and lowest water level. Add ¼ cup of laundry detergent and an old pair of jeans for agitation. Check piece every 5–10 minutes, agitating until stitches are not seen and rug measures 24" x 34½"/61 x 87.5cm; approx 28–30 minutes. Rinse in cold water; do not allow to go through spin cycle. Remove from pillowcase, then gently roll in towels to assist in drying if rug is extremely wet. Hand-block to measurements. Let air dry flat for 1 to 2 days.

PLACEMENT DIAGRAM

MC, D, A, MC 1	MC, B, E, MC 2	MC, C, D, MC 3	MC, A, B, MC 4	MC, E, C, MC 5	MC, D, A, MC 1	MC, B, E, MC 2
MC, A, B, MC 4	MC, E, C, MC 5	MC, A, B, MC 4	MC, D, A, MC 1	MC, B, E, MC 2	MC, C, D, MC 3	MC, D, A, MC 1
MC, E, C, MC 5	MC, C, D, MC 3	MC, D, A, MC 1	MC, B, E, MC 2	MC, A, B, MC 4	MC, E, C, MC 5	MC, C, D, MC 3
MC, B, E, MC 2	MC, E, C, MC 5	MC, A, B, MC 4	MC, C, D, MC 3	MC, D, A, MC 1	MC, B, E, MC 2	MC, E, C, MC 5
MC, C, D, MC 3	MC, A, B, MC 4	MC, D, A, MC 1	MC, B, E, MC 2	MC, E, C, MC 5	MC, C, D, MC 3	MC, A, B, MC 4

■■■□

Go green with this all-natural, reusable tote bag. Felting creates a durable fabric that won't stretch out even with a heavy load. Designed by Leslie Johnson in a bright array of candy colors.

FINISHED MEASUREMENTS

■ Approx 12½"/31.5cm wide x 14"/35.5cm high x 3¾"/9.5cm deep (excluding handles)

MATERIALS

■ 2 4oz/113g skeins (each approx 190yd/174m) of Brown Sheep Company *Lamb's Pride Worsted* (wool/mohair) in #M120 limeade (A) 🔳

■ 1 skein each in #M105 RPM pink (B), #M110 orange you glad (C) and #M38 lotus pink (D)

■ Size J/10 (6mm) crochet hook *or size to obtain gauge*

■ Two 12½"/31.5cm wide x 14"/35.5cm high x 2"/5cm deep sheets of Styrofoam

■ One 12" x 18"/30.5 x 45.5cm sheet of plastic canvas

■ ½yd/.5m lining fabric and matching sewing thread (optional)

GAUGE

11 sts and 10 rows to 4"/10cm over hdc using size I/9 (5.5mm) crochet hook (before felting).
Take time to check gauge.

Notes

1 When changing colors, draw new color through 3 lps on hook to complete last st.

2 To join yarn with a hdc, make a slip knot and place on hook. Yo, insert hook into st, yo and draw up a lp, yo and draw through all 3 lps on hook.

STITCH GLOSSARY

hdc2tog [Yo, insert hook in next st, yo and draw up a lp] twice, yo and draw through all 5 lps on hook.

TOTE

Bottom

With A, ch 50.

Row I (RS) Hdc in 3rd ch from hook and in each ch across—48 sts. Turn.

Rows 2–7 Ch 2 (does not count as hdc), hdc in each st across. Turn.

Row 8 Ch 2, hdc in each st across, changing to B. Turn.

Sides

Rnd I (RS) Ch 2 (does not count as a hdc), hdc in each st across, turn to side edge, work 2 hdc in side edge of first row, work 7 hdc evenly spaced across to last row, work 2 hdc in side edge of last row, turn to bottom lps of foundation ch, hdc in each bottom lp across, turn to side edge, work 2 hdc in side edge of first row, work 7 hdc evenly spaced across to last row, work 2 hdc in side edge of last row, join rnd with a sl st in top of beg ch-2—118 sts. Ch 2, turn.

Rnds 2–7 Hdc in each st around, join rnd with a sl st in top of beg ch-2. Ch 2, turn.

Rnd 8 Hdc in each st around, join rnd with a sl st in top of beg ch-2 changing to C. Ch 2, turn.

Rnds 9–13 Rep rnd 2.

Rnd 14 Hdc in each st around, join rnd with a sl st in top of beg ch-2 changing to D. Ch 2, turn.

Rnds 15–17 Rep rnd 2.

Rnd 18 Hdc in each st around, join rnd with a sl st in top of beg ch-2 changing to B. Ch 2, turn.

Rnd 19 Rep rnd 2.

Rnd 20 Hdc in each st around, join rnd with a sl st in top of beg ch-2 changing to C. Ch 2, turn.

Rnds 21–23 Rep rnd 2.

Rnd 24 Hdc in each st around, join rnd with a sl st in top of beg ch-2 changing to D. Ch 2, turn.

Rnds 25–29 Rep rnd 2.

Rnd 30 Hdc in each st around, join rnd with a sl st in top of beg ch-2 changing to B. Ch 2, turn.

Rnds 31–33 Rep rnd 2.

Rnd 34 Hdc in each st around, join rnd with a sl st in top of beg ch-2 changing to C. Ch 2, turn.

Rnd 35 Rep rnd 2.

Rnd 36 Hdc in each st around, join rnd with a sl st in top of beg ch-2 changing to A. Ch 2, turn.

Top band

Rnds 37–40 Hdc in each st around, join rnd with a sl st in top of beg ch-2. Ch 2, turn.

Rnd 41 Hdc in first 9 sts, ch 5, skip next 5 sts (strap opening), hdc in next 20 sts, ch 5, skip next 5 sts, hdc in next 29 sts, ch 5, skip next 5 sts, hdc in next 20 sts, ch 5, skip next 5 sts, hdc in last 20 sts, join rnd with a sl st in top of beg ch-2. Ch 2, turn.

Rnd 42 Hdc in each st around, working 5 hdc in each ch-5 lp, join rnd with a sl st in top of beg ch-2. Ch 2, turn.

Rnds 43 and 44 Rep rnd 37. When rnd 44 is completed, fasten off.

Straps (make 2)

With A, ch 7, leaving a long tail for sewing.

Row 1 (RS) Hdc in 3rd ch from hook and in each ch across–5 sts. Ch 2, turn.

Rows 2–40 Hdc in each st across. Mark beg and end of last row. Ch 2, turn.

Row 41 Work 2 hdc in first st, hdc in next 3 sts, work 2 hdc in last st—7 sts. Ch 2, turn.

Rows 42–89 Hdc in each st across. Ch 2, turn.

Row 90 Hdc2tog, hdc in next 3 sts, hdc2tog—5 sts. Mark beg and end of last row. Ch 2, turn.

Rows 91–130 Hdc in each st across. Ch 2, turn. When row 130 is completed, fasten off leaving a long tail for sewing.

For each strap, fold in half, WS facing. Sc strap tog between markers to form handles.

On front of tote, slip strap through both openings in top band. Beg at bottom edge, pin strap in place making sure it is perfectly parallel to side edges. Use tails to whipstitch bottom edge of strap to edge of last A row on bottom. Sew straps in place using A. Rep on back of tote with rem strap. Fold top band in half to RS along rnd 41. Sew in place.

Felting

Place tote in a zippered pillowcase and put into washing machine. Use hot-water wash, a regular (not delicate) cycle and lowest water level. Add ¼ cup of laundry detergent and an old pair of jeans for agitation. Check piece every 5–10 minutes, until tote measures 12½"/31.5cm wide x 14"/35.5cm high x 3¾"/9.5cm deep. Rinse in cold water; do not allow to go through spin cycle. Remove from pillowcase, then gently roll in towels to assist in drying. Hand-block to measurements. Insert both sheets of Styrofoam so tote dries to shape. Place on flat surface, arranging handles so they are smooth and straight. Let air dry flat for 1 to 2 days, turning every 6–8 hours for even drying. Cut 2 pieces of plastic canvas to fit inside bottom of tote. Working through all layers, sew double thickness of plastic canvas to inside bottom of tote using A.

Lining

Measure inside circumference of tote, then add 1"/2.5cm for seam allowance. Cut one strip of fabric 18"/45.5cm by total circumference measurement. Fold strip in half lengthwise. Using a ½"/1.3cm seam allowance throughout, sew seam. Press seam open. With RS together, position seam in center of a side; press. Sew bottom seam. Insert lining into tote. Turn and pin top edge of lining to WS so top edge of lining is even with bottom edge of top band. Remove lining; press. Trim top edge seam allowance to ½"/1.3cm if necessary. Insert lining into tote. Slipstitch top edge of lining in place using sewing thread.

Happy feet

■■■▢

Everyone's favorite cold-weather friend gets the royal felting treatment from the top of his adorable head to the bottom of his webbed feet. Designed by Kathleen Stuart, he's worked in the round in basic single crochet.

FINISHED MEASUREMENTS
■ Approx 12"/30.5cm tall

MATERIALS
■ 2 3oz/85g skeins (each approx 158yd/144m) of Lion Brand Yarn *Lion Wool* (wool) in #153 ebony (MC) ▣
■ 1 skein each in #099 winter white (A) and #133 pumpkin (B)
■ Size H/8 (5mm) crochet hook *or size to obtain gauge*
■ Polyester fiberfill
■ Small safety pin

GAUGE
14 sts and 17 rnds to 4"/10cm over sc using size H/8 (5mm) crochet hook (before felting). *Take time to check gauge.*

Notes

1 When changing colors, draw new color through last 2 lps on hook to complete last st.
2 To join yarn with a sc, make a slip knot and place on hook. Insert hook into st, yo and draw up a lp, yo and draw through both lps on hook.

STITCH GLOSSARY
sc2tog [Insert hook in next st, yo and draw up a lp] twice, yo and draw through all 3 lps on hook.

Ssc (spike single crochet) Insert hook between next 2 sts of row 1, yo and draw up a lp that is the same height as the working row, yo and draw through both lps on hook.

Sss (spike slip stitch) Insert hook between next 2 sts of row 1, yo and draw up a lp that is the same height as the working row, then draw through lp on hook.

PENGUIN

Head

With MC, ch 2.

Rnd 1 (RS) Work 6 sc in 2nd ch from hook. Mark last st made with the safety pin. You will be working in a spiral marking the last st made with the safety pin to indicate end of rnd.

Rnd 2 Work 2 sc in each st around—12 sts.

Rnd 3 [Sc in next st, work 2 sc in next st] 6 times—18 sts.

Rnd 4 [Sc in next 2 sts, work 2 sc in next st] 6 times—24 sts.

Rnd 5 [Sc in next 3 sts, work 2 sc in next st] 6 times—30 sts.

Rnd 6 [Sc in next 4 sts, work 2 sc in next st] 6 times—36 sts.

Rnd 7 [Sc in next 5 sts, work 2 sc in next st] 6 times—42 sts.

Rnd 8 [Sc in next 6 sts, work 2 sc in next st] 6 times—48 sts.

Rnds 9–18 Sc in each st around.

Rnd 19 [Sc in next 6 sts, sc2tog] 6 times—42 sts.

Rnd 20 [Sc in next 5 sts, sc2tog] 6 times—36 sts.

Rnd 21 [Sc in next 4 sts, sc2tog] 6 times—30 sts.

Rnd 22 [Sc in next 3 sts, sc2tog] 6 times—24 sts.

Rnd 23 [Sc in next 2 sts, sc2tog] 6 times—18 sts. Stuff head with fiberfill.

Rnd 24 [Sc in next 2 sts, work 2 sc in next st] 6 times—24 sts. Drop safety pin. You will now be working in joined rnds that are worked back and forth.

Body

Rnd 25 [Sc in next 3 sts, work 2 sc in next st] 4 times changing to A, [sc in next 3 sts, work 2 sc in next st] twice, join rnd with a sl st in first sc—30 sts. Turn.

Rnd 26 Ch 1, [sc in next 4 sts, work 2 sc in next st] twice changing to MC, [sc in next 4 sts, work 2 sc in next st] 4 times, join rnd with a sl st in first sc—36 sts. Turn.

Rnd 27 [Sc in next 5 sts, work 2 sc in next st] 4 times changing to A, [sc in next 5 sts, work 2 sc in next st] twice, join rnd with a sl st in first sc—42 sts. Turn.

Rnd 28 Ch 1, [sc in next 6 sts, work 2 sc in next st] twice changing to MC, [sc in next 6 sts, work 2 sc in next st] 4 times, join rnd with a sl st in first sc—48 sts. Turn.

Rnd 29 Ch 1, [sc in next 7 sts, work 2 sc in next st] 4 times changing to A, [sc in next 7 sts, work 2 sc in next st] twice, join rnd with a sl st in first sc—54 sts. Turn.

Rnd 30 Ch 1, [sc in next 8 sts, work 2 sc in next st] twice changing to MC, [sc in next 8 sts, work 2 sc in next st] 4 times, join rnd with a sl st in first sc—60 sts. Turn.

Rnd 31 Ch 1, sc in first 40 sts changing to A, sc in last 20 sts, join rnd with a sl st in first sc. Turn.

Rnd 32 Ch 1, sc in first 20 sts changing to MC, sc in last 40 sts, join rnd with a sl st in first sc.

Rnds 33–53 Rep rnds 31 and 32 10 times, then row 31 once. Turn.

Tail

Rnd 54 Ch 1, sc in first 20 sts changing to MC, sc in next 17 sts, hdc in next st, work 2 dc in next st, work 2 tr in next 2 sts, work 2 dc in next st, hdc in next st, sc in last 17 sts, join rnd with a sl st in first sc—64 sts. Turn.

Rnd 55 Ch 1, sc in first 21 sts, work 2 sc in next 2 sts, sc in next 21 sts changing to A, sc in last 20 sts, join rnd with a sl st in first sc—66 sts. Turn.

Rnd 56 Ch 1, sc in first 20 sts changing to MC, sc in next 17 sts, [sc2tog] 6 times, sc in last 17 sts, join rnd with a sl st in first sc—60 sts. Turn.

Rnd 57 Ch 1, [sc in next 8 sts, sc2tog] 4 times changing to A, [sc in next 8 sts, sc2tog] twice, join rnd with a sl st in first sc—54 sts. Turn.

Rnd 58 Ch 1, [sc in next 7 sts, sc2tog] twice changing to MC, [sc in next 7 sts, sc2tog] 4 times, join rnd with a sl st in first sc—48 sts. Turn.

Rnd 59 Ch 1, [sc in next 6 sts, sc2tog] 4 times changing to A, [sc in next 6 sts, sc2tog] twice, join rnd with a sl st in first sc—42 sts. Turn.

Rnd 60 Ch 1, [sc in next 5 sts, sc2tog] twice changing to MC, [sc in next 5 sts, sc2tog] 4 times, join rnd with a sl st in first sc—36 sts. Turn.

Rnd 61 Ch 1, [sc in next 4 sts, sc2tog] 4 times changing to A, [sc in next 4 sts, sc2tog] twice, join rnd with a sl st in first sc—30 sts. Turn.

Rnd 62 Ch 1, [sc in next 3 sts, sc2tog] twice changing to MC, [sc in next 3 sts, sc2tog] 4 times, join rnd with a sl st in first sc—24 sts. Do not turn. Cut A and cont to work unjoined rnds with MC as foll:

Rnd 63 Ch 1, beg in same st as joining, work as foll: [sc in next 2 sts, sc2tog] 6 times—18 sts. Stuff body with fiberfill.

Rnd 64 [Sc in next st, sc2tog] 6 times—12 sts.

Rnd 65 [Sc2tog] 6 times—6 sts. Fasten off.

Wings (make 2 pieces)

Beg at bottom, with MC, ch 2.

Rnd 1 (RS) Work 6 sc in 2nd ch from hook. Mark last st made with the safety pin. You will be working in a spiral marking the last st made with the safety pin to indicate end of rnd.

Rnd 2 [Sc in next st, work 2 sc in next st] 3 times—9 sts.

Rnd 3 [Sc in next 2 sts, work 2 sc in next st] 3 times—12 sts.

Rnd 4 [Sc in next 3 sts, work 2 sc in next st] 3 times—15 sts.

Rnd 5 [Sc in next 4 sts, work 2 sc in next st] 3 times—18 sts.

Rnd 6 [Sc in next 5 sts, work 2 sc in next st] 3 times—21 sts.

Rnd 7 [Sc in next 6 sts, work 2 sc in next st] 3 times—24 sts.

Rnds 8–20 Sc in each st around.

Rnd 21 [Sc in next 2 sts, sc2tog] 6 times—18 sts.

Rnd 22 [Sc in next st, sc2tog] 6 times—12 sts.

Rnd 23 [Sc2tog] 6 times—6 sts. Fasten off leaving a long tail for sewing.

Beak and Eye Patches

With B, ch 2.

Rnd 1 (RS) Work 6 sc in 2nd ch from hook. Mark last st made with the safety pin. You will be working in a spiral marking the last st made with the safety pin to indicate end of rnd.

Rnd 2 [Sc in next st, work 2 sc in next st] 3 times—9 sts.

Rnd 3 Sc in each st around.

Rnd 4 [Sc in next 2 sts, work 2 sc in next st] 3 times—12 sts.

Rnd 5 Sc in each st around changing to A

in last st. Fasten off, leaving a long tail for sewing.

Left eye patch

Row 1 (RS) Sc in first st, work 2 sc in next st—3 sts. Turn.

Row 2 Ch 3 (counts as 1 dc), dc in first 2 sts, work 2 dc in last st—5 sts. Turn.

Row 3 Ch 3 (counts as 1 dc), dc in first 4 sts, work 2 dc in last st—7 sts. Fasten off leaving a long tail for sewing.

Right eye patch

Row 1 (RS) With RS facing, skip 1 st after left eye patch, join A with a sc in next st, work 2 sc in next st—3 sts. Turn. Beg with row 2, cont to work same as left eye patch.

Feet (make 4 pieces)

With B, ch 5.

Row 1 (RS) Sc in 2nd ch from hook and in each ch across—4 sts. Turn.

Row 2 Ch 1, sc in each st across. Turn.

Row 3 Ch 1, sc in first st, ch 3, hdc in 2nd ch from hook and in next ch, work Ssc; ch 4, hdc in 2nd ch from hook and in next 2 ch, work Ssc; ch 3, hdc in 2nd ch from hook and in next ch, work (Ssc, Sss). Fasten off leaving a long tail for sewing.

FINISHING

Flatten each wing. Position and pin top open edge of wing to side of penguin, so top edge is even with rnd 27. Whipstitch top edge in place using MC, closing opening at the same time. For each foot, place 2 feet tog, WS facing. Whipstitch edges tog using B. Position and pin straight edge of each foot to bottom of penguin, so straight edge is even with rnd 61 and toes face forward. Whipstitch each straight edge in place using B. Position and pin beak/eye patches to face, so beak is on rnd 14, and beak/eye patches are centered side to side. Whipstitch beak using B and eye patches using A.

Felting

Place penguin in a zippered pillowcase and put into washing machine. Use hot-water wash and a regular (not delicate) cycle. Add ¼ cup of laundry detergent and an old pair of jeans for agitation. Check frequently until penguin measures 12"/30.5cm tall. Rinse in cold water and remove from pillowcase. Shape body, wings, beak and feet, then allow to air dry.

Embroidery

Embroider vertical satin stitch eyes using MC.

Ice 'n roses

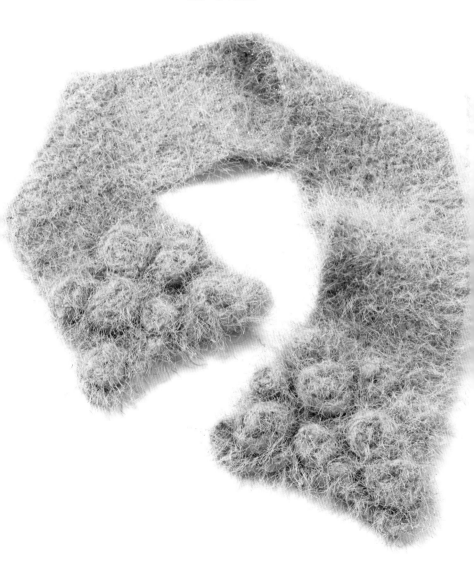

Put some glitz into felting when you combine wool and metallic eyelash yarns. Monica Brown has paired two yarns of nearly the same color to create a ritzy scarf that's adorned with lots of easy-to-make rosettes.

FINISHED MEASUREMENTS

■ Approx 5"/12.5cm wide x 36"/90cm long

MATERIALS

■ 3 1.75oz/50g balls (each approx 102yd/95m) of Crystal Palace *Aran* (wool) in #1008 soft blue (A) (4)

■ 3 1.75oz/50g balls (each approx 120yd/110m) of Crystal Palace *Fizz Stardust* (polyester/soft metallic fiber) in #4197 periwinkle (B) (3)

■ Size M/13 (9mm) crochet hook *or size needed to obtain gauge*

GAUGE

10 sts and 7 rows to 4"/10cm over hdc using size M/13 (9mm) crochet hook with 1 strand each of A and B held tog (before felting). *Take time to check gauge.*

Notes

1 Use 1 strand each of A and B held tog throughout.

2 To join yarn with a hdc, make a slip knot and place on hook. Yo, insert hook into st, yo and draw up a lp, yo and draw through both 3 lps on hook.

SCARF

First half

With 1 strand each of A and B held tog, loosely ch 19.

Row 1 (RS) Hdc in 3rd ch from hook and in each ch across—17 sts. Turn.

Row 2 Ch 2, hdc in each st across. Turn. Rep row 2 until piece measures 18½"/47cm from beg. Turn.

Edging

Next row Ch 3, work 2 dc in first st, sc in next st, *work 3 dc in next st, sc in next st; rep from * to end. Fasten off.

Second half

Position first half of scarf so RS is facing and bottom lps of foundation ch are at top.

Row 1 (RS) With 1 strand each of A and B held tog, join yarns with a hdc in first bottom lp, hdc in next 16 bottom lps—17 sts. Beg with row 2, cont to work as for first half.

LARGE ROSETTE (MAKE 7 PIECES)

With 1 strand each of A and B held tog, loosely ch 12.

Row 1 (RS) Hdc in 3rd ch from hook and in each ch across—10 sts. Turn.

Row 2 Ch 2, work 2 hdc in each st across—20 sts. Fasten off leaving a long tail for sewing.

SMALL ROSETTE (MAKE 10 PIECES)

With 1 strand each of A and B held tog, loosely ch 7.

Row 1 (RS) Hdc in 3rd ch from hook and in each ch across—5 sts. Turn.

Row 2 Ch 2, work 2 hdc in each st across—10 sts. Fasten off leaving a long tail for sewing.

FINISHING

To form each rosette, coil crocheted strip into flower shape. On WS, use one tail to sew center tog to secure rosette shape. On RS of scarf, arrange and pin 3 large and 5 small rosettes on one half of scarf, and 4 large and 5 small on the opposite half. Do not pack arrangement too tightly as the rosettes will be closer tog after felting. For each rosette, use rem tail to sew center and outside edges in place.

Felting

Place scarf in a zippered pillowcase and put into washing machine. Use hot-water wash, a regular (not delicate) cycle and the lowest water level. Add a tablespoon of laundry detergent and two large beach towels to assist agitation. Agitate twice checking measurements and stopping before spin cycle. Repeat process until scarf measures 36"/90cm long x 5"/12.5cm wide. Gently roll scarf in towels to assist in drying if scarf is extremely wet. Hand block scarf into shape. Let air dry flat.

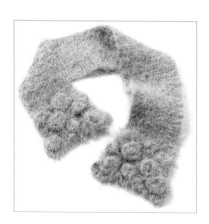

Hold it right there!

Marty Miller has come up with the perfect solution to the age-old problem of not enough storage. Her soft-sided baskets can be used to hold everything from cosmetics to small toys. The round-bottomed baskets are worked in single crochet, while the square-bottomed baskets are worked à la classic granny.

FINISHED MEASUREMENTS
Round-bottomed basket
■ Approx 6¾"/17cm diameter x 6"/15cm high
Square-bottomed basket
■ Approx 6½"/16.5cm wide x 5"/12.5cm high

MATERIALS
Round-bottomed or square-bottomed basket
■ 2 1.75oz/50g balls (each approx 110yd/101m) of Noro/Knitting Fever, Inc. *Kureyon* (wool) in #182 or #183 **(4)**
■ Size L/11 (8mm) crochet hook *or size to obtain gauge*
■ Small safety pin

GAUGE
Round-bottomed basket
9 sts and 12 rnds to 4"/10cm over sc using size L/11 (8mm) crochet hook (before felting).
Square-bottomed basket
Gauge is not important.
Take time to check gauge.

ROUND-BOTTOMED BASKET
Ch 2.

Rnd 1 (RS) Work 6 sc in 2nd ch from hook. Mark last st made with the safety pin. You will be working in a spiral marking the last st made with the safety pin to indicate end of rnd.

Rnd 2 Work 2 sc in each st around—12 sts.

Rnd 3 [Sc in next st, work 2 sc in next st] 6 times—18 sts.

Rnd 4 [Sc in next 2 sts, work 2 sc in next st] 6 times—24 sts.

Rnd 5 [Sc in next 3 sts, work 2 sc in next st] 6 times—30 sts.

Rnd 6 [Sc in next 4 sts, work 2 sc in next st] 6 times—36 sts.

Rnd 7 [Sc in next 5 sts, work 2 sc in next st] 6 times—42 sts.

Rnd 8 [Sc in next 6 sts, work 2 sc in next st] 6 times—48 sts.

Rnd 9 [Sc in next 7 sts, work 2 sc in next st] 6 times—54 sts.

Rnd 10 [Sc in next 8 sts, work 2 sc in next st] 6 times—60 sts.

Rnd 11 [Sc in next 9 sts, work 2 sc in next st] 6 times—66 sts.

Rnd 12 [Sc in next 10 sts, work 2 sc in next st] 6 times—72 sts.

Rnd 13 Working in back lps only, sc in each sc around.

Rnd 14 Sc in each st around. Rep rnd 14 until piece measures 9"/23cm from rnd 12 or until you run out of yarn. Fasten off.

SQUARE-BOTTOMED BASKET

Ch 4. Join ch with a sl st forming a ring.

Rnd 1 (RS) Ch 3 (counts as 1 dc), work 2 dc in ring, ch 1, [work 3 dc in ring, ch 1] 3 times, join rnd with a sl st in top of beg ch-3—12 dc and 4 ch-1 sps.

Rnd 2 Sl st in each st to first ch-1 sp, ch 3 (counts as 1 dc), work (2 dc, ch 1, 3 dc) in same ch-1 sp (beg corner made), ch 1, [work (3 dc, ch 1, 3 dc) in next ch-1 sp (corner made), ch 1] 3 times, join rnd with a sl st in top of beg ch-3—4 corner ch-1 sps.

Rnd 3 Sl st in each st to first corner ch-1 sp, ch 3 (counts as 1 dc), work (2 dc, ch 1, 3 dc) in same ch-1 sp, ch 1, work 3 dc in next ch-1 sp, ch 1, *work (3 dc, ch 1, 3 dc) in next corner ch-1 sp, ch 1, work 3 dc in next ch-1 sp, ch 1; rep from * around twice more, join rnd with a sl st in top of beg ch-3.

Rnd 4 Sl st in each st to first corner ch-1 sp, ch 3 (counts as 1 dc), work (2 dc, ch 1, 3 dc) in same ch-1 sp, ch 1, [work 3 dc in next ch-1 sp, ch 1] twice, *work (3 dc, ch 1, 3 dc) in next corner ch-1 sp, ch 1, [work 3 dc in next ch-1 sp, ch 1] twice; rep from * around twice more, join rnd with a sl st in top of beg ch-3.

Rnd 5 Sl st in each st to first corner ch-1 sp, ch 3 (counts as 1 dc), work (2 dc, ch 1, 3 dc) in same ch-1 sp, ch 1, [work 3 dc in next ch-1 sp, ch 1] 3 times, *work (3 dc, ch 1, 3 dc) in next corner ch-1 sp, ch 1, [work 3 dc in next ch-1 sp, ch 1] 3 times; rep from * around twice more, join rnd with a sl st in top of beg ch-3.

Rnds 6–14 Sl st in each st to first corner ch-1 sp, ch 3 (counts as 1 dc), work 2 dc in same ch-1 sp, ch 1, *work 3 dc in next ch-1 sp, ch 1; rep from * around, join rnd with a sl st in top of beg ch-3.

Rnd 15 Ch 1, sc in same sp as joining, cont to sc in each dc around, skipping all ch-1 sps, join rnd with a sl st in first sc. Fasten off.

FINISHING

Felting

Place each basket in a separate zippered pillowcase. Set the water level on your washing machine to low, and the temperature to hot. Put in a little clear laundry detergent, an old towel or two (or a pair of old jeans, or a couple of rubber balls or flip flops) to help with agitation. Set your washer for a heavy load, and check the felting progress every 5 or 10 minutes. Do not let the baskets go through the spin cycle, as this may cause creasing. You may have to repeat this felting process one or more times to adequately felt the baskets. If so, drain the water from the washing machine each time, and start again. You may also add some boiling water to the machine. When fully felted, the round basket should measure approx 6¾"/17cm diameter x 6"/15cm high and square basket 6½"/16.5cm wide x 5"/12.5cm high x 6½"/16.5cm deep. Rinse them in cold water, then roll them in towels to squeeze out the excess water. Stretch the baskets into shape, stuffing them with newspaper to wick away the water and help them dry. Let air dry on a flat surface.

Dear diary

Write down all your warm and fuzzy thoughts in this heartfelt journal that you make from scratch. Vashti Braha created this delightful pink-on-pink striped cover that gets a cut-fringe edging after felting.

FINISHED MEASUREMENTS
■ Approx 9"/23cm wide x 11"/28cm high (including fringe)

MATERIALS
■ 1 3.5oz/100g skein (each approx 193yd/176m) of Louet North America *Riverstone Worsted* (wool) each in #26 crabapple (A) and #51 pink panther (B) ⬛

■ Size K/10½ (6.5mm) crochet hook or size to obtain gauge
■ One 9" x 16"/23 x 40.5cm piece of white cardstock
■ Forty-eight 8½" x 14"/21.5cm x 35.5cm sheets of white paper
■ Blocking board and pins
■ Awl or ice pick
■ Large-eyed yarn needle
■ Fabric glue
■ ½"/6mm flat paintbrush

GAUGE
13 sts and 7 rows to 4"/10cm over hdc using size K/10½ (6.5mm) crochet hook (before felting).
Take time to check gauge.

Notes

1 The loose gauge will give the sts an uneven appearance, but this will be corrected during the felting and blocking process.

2 When changing colors, draw new color through sl st when joining rnd.

COVER

With of A, ch 24.

Foundation row (WS) Sc in 2nd ch from hook and in each ch across—23 sts. Turn.

Rnd 1 (RS) Ch 2 (counts as 1 hdc), hdc in each st across, turn to side edge of row, work (4 hdc, ch 1, hdc, ch 1, 4 hdc) in side edge of row, turn to bottom lps of foundation ch, hdc in each bottom lp across, turn to side edge of row, work (4 hdc, ch 1, hdc, ch 1, 3 hdc) in side edge, join rnd with a sl st in top of beg ch-2 changing to B—64 sts and 4 ch. Turn. (**Note** On rnd 2, ch are treated as sts.) Cont to work in front lp only of each st around as foll:

Rnd 2 Ch 2 (counts as 1 hdc), work 3 hdc in next st, *hdc in next 3 sts, work 3 hdc in next 2 sts, hdc in next 27 sts*, work 3 hdc in next 2 sts; rep from * to *, end work 3 hdc in last st, join rnd with a sl st in top of beg ch-2—84 sts. Turn.

Rnd 3 Ch 2 (counts as 1 hdc), work 2 hdc in same place as joining, *hdc in 31 sts, work 3 hdc in next 2 sts, hdc in next 7 sts*, work 3 hdc in next 2 sts; rep from * to *, end work 3 hdc in last st, join rnd with a sl st in top of beg ch-2 changing to A—100 sts. Turn.

Rnd 4 Ch 2 (counts as 1 hdc), work 3 hdc in first st, *hdc in next 11 sts, work 3 hdc in next 2 sts, hdc in next 35 sts*, work 3 hdc in next 2 sts; rep from * to *, end work 3 hdc in last st, join rnd with a sl st in top of beg ch-2—116 sts. Turn.

Rnd 5 Ch 2 (counts as 1 hdc), work 2 hdc in same place as joining, *hdc in next 39 sts, work 3 hdc in next 2 sts, hdc in next 15 sts*, work 3 hdc in next 2 sts; rep from * to *, end work 3 hdc in last st, join rnd with a sl st in top of beg ch-2 changing to B—132 sts. Turn.

Rnds 6–13 Rep rnds 2–5 twice more, working 4 more sts between incs on each side of rectangle every rnd—260 sts.

Rnds 14–16 Rep rnds 2–4 once more, working 4 more sts between incs on each side of rectangle every rnd and changing colors every rnd—308 sts.

Rnd 17 Ch 2 (counts as 1 hdc), hdc in same place as joining, *skip next st, hdc in next; rep from * across each side, working 1 hdc in each of 4 sts at each corner, join rnd with a sl st in top of beg ch-2 changing to A. (**Note** An exact st count is unnecessary as reducing the number of sts by roughly half will improve the shape when felted.)

Rnd 18 Ch 2 (counts as 1 hdc), hdc in each st around, join rnd with a sl st changing to B. Turn.

Rnd 19 Ch 2 (counts as 1 hdc), hdc in each st around, working 3 hdc in each corner, join rnd with a sl st in top of beg ch-2. Fasten off.

Felting

Felt journal cover in washing machine set to hot water regular cycle and spin. Add a small amount of laundry soap and a few colorfast, no-lint items such as kitchen dish towels and white t-shirts to aid the felting process with gentle friction. If cover is not felted tightly enough to obscure the stitches, repeat cycle. Pin damp journal cover to blocking board so it is a rectangle and stripes are straight. (**Note** Cover will likely be larger than finished measurements, but can be cut down to size when dry.) Let air dry 1 to 2 days. If necessary, trim to measure 18"/45.5cm wide x 11"/28cm high.

Assembling

Fold sheets of paper in half, then stack together. With the awl, poke 3 holes along fold with the first ¾"/2cm from top edge, the last ¾"/2cm from bottom edge and the remaining hole spaced evenly between. Enlarge holes with yarn needle. Do not fold cardstock, instead measure and mark for center, then mark for holes with the first 1"/2.5cm from top edge, the last 1"/2.5cm from bottom edge and the remaining hole spaced evenly between. Use awl to poke holes, then enlarge holes with yarn needle. Use paintbrush to apply glue evenly to WS of cardstock. Adhere to WS of journal cover taking care to center top to bottom and side to side. Close journal cover, inserting folded pages. Place a book on top, then allow to dry overnight. Taking care not to cut cardstock, cut 1"/2.5cm wide by 1"/2.5cm deep fringe all around edge, angling cuts around corners. Cut 4 A and 2 B strands of yarn 60"/152.5cm long. Loosely braid the strands together. Thread one end of braid in yarn needle.

From RS, insert needle through bottom hole of journal cover; remove needle. Thread opposite end of braid in yarn needle. From RS, insert needle through top hole; remove needle. On WS, even up braid ends. Thread both ends of braid in yarn needle. From WS, insert needle through center hole; remove needle. Undo braid, then divide strands again into 2 groups of 6 strands. Working more tightly. braid each group of strands to within last 2"/5cm. Make a overhand knot 2"/5cm from ends. Position loose braid that runs from top hole to bottom hole between braided ends, then tie braids once to secure.

Stripe 'n carry

■■■▢

It's quite magical how a simple afghan stitch stripe becomes subtle diagonal pinstripes on one side and bold horizontal stripes on the flip side when felted. Donna Childs did the trick to make this extra-roomy shoulder bag extra-special.

FINISHED MEASUREMENTS
■ Approx 15½"/39.5cm wide x 14"/35.5 high x 3"/7.5cm deep (excluding strap)

MATERIALS
■ 2 8oz/227g hanks (each approx 500yd/457m) of Lorna's Laces *Fisherman* (wool) in #16ns charcoal (A) ▨
■ 1 hank each in #47n carol green (B) and #207 envy (C)
■ Size I/9 (5.5mm) afghan hook *or size to obtain gauge*
■ Size I/9 (5.5mm) crochet hook *or size to obtain gauge*

GAUGE
16 sts and 16 rows to 4"/10cm over afghan st using size I/9 (5.5mm) afghan hook (before felting).
Take time to check gauge.

Note

Each row of afghan st is worked in two halves. The first half is worked from right to left and the second half is worked from left to right.

FRONT

With A, ch 91.

Row 1 (first half) Retaining all lps on hook, insert hook into 2nd ch from hook, yo and draw up a lp, *insert hook into next ch, yo and draw up a lp; rep from * across—91 lps on hook. Do not turn. Change to B.

Row 1 (second half) With B, yo, draw through first lp on hook, *yo and draw through next 2 lps on hook; rep from * until 1 lp rem on hook. Do not turn. Change to A.

Row 2 (first half) With B, insert hook under 2nd vertical thread from side edge of the previous row, yo and draw up a lp, retaining all lps on hook, draw up a lp in each vertical thread across. Change to A.

Row 2 (second half) With A, yo, draw through first lp on hook, * yo and draw through 2 lps on hook; rep from * across. Do not turn.

Row 3 (first half) With A, insert hook under 2nd vertical thread from side edge of the previous row, yo and draw up a lp, retaining all lps on hook, draw up a lp in each vertical thread across. Change to B.

Row 3 (second half) With B, yo, draw through first lp on hook, * yo and draw through 2 lps on hook; rep from * across. Do not turn. Change to A. Rep rows 2 and 3 (first and second halves) for afghan st until piece measures 17½"/44.5cm from beg, end with second half of row 2. Place lp on afghan hook onto crochet hook. Ch 1, turn to side edge.

Edging

Rnd 1 (WS) With A, sc in each st and row around, working 3 sc in each corner, join rnd with a sl st in first st. Fasten off.

BACK AND FRONT FLAP

Work as for front, using C instead of B. Work until piece measures 32"/81cm from beg, end with second half of row 2. Place lp on afghan hook onto crochet hook. Ch 1, turn to side edge. Work edging as for front.

STRAP/GUSSETS

With A and crochet hook, ch 17.

Row 1 (RS) Dc in 4th ch from hook and in each ch across—15 sts. Turn.

Row 2 Ch 3 (counts as dc), dc in each st across. Turn. Rep row 2 until piece measures 120"/305cm from beg. Fasten off leaving a long tail for sewing.

FINISHING

Sew the two short edges of strap tog using tail. With WS tog, pin strap/gusset seam to center bottom of front. Cont to pin strap/gussets along bottom edge, then up side edges. With RS of front facing, crochet hook and A, beg at top edge and sc front and strap/gussets tog. Fasten off. With WS tog, pin strap/gusset seam to center bottom of back. Cont to pin strap/gussets along bottom edge, then up side edges to same point as front. With RS of back facing, sc back and strap/gussets tog beg at same point as front seam. Fasten off.

Felting

Machine wash and dry bag until it measures 15½"/39.5cm wide x 14"/35.5 high x 3"/7.5cm deep. Block bag between two damp pressing cloths using a hot iron.

Tea rose

■■□▭

Linda Cyr has turned the practical tea cozy into a colorful work of art. The cozy features a top loop, multicolor looped posy and shapely leaves. What prettier way can you think of to keep your tea piping hot?

FINISHED MEASUREMENTS

■ Approx 9"/23cm in diameter at base x 9¼"/23.5cm high (excluding top loop)

MATERIALS

■ 2 3.5oz/100g balls (each approx 210yd/ 192m) of Plymouth Yarn Co. *Galway Worsted* (wool) in #129 blue (MC) (**4**)

■ 1 ball each in #91 pumpkin (A), #154 tangerine (B) and #130 grass (C)

■ Size J/10 (6mm) crochet hook *or size to obtain gauge*

■ Sewing thread to match flower and leaves

■ Sewing needle

■ Small safety pin

GAUGE

12 sts and 14 rnds to 4"/10cm over sc using size J/10 (6mm) crochet hook (before felting). *Take time to check gauge.*

Note

Tea cozy shown fits a 6–cup teapot. You can achieve the right size to fit your teapot during the felting process.

COZY

Top loop

With MC, ch 14. Join ch with a sl st forming a ring.

Body

Ch 2.

Rnd 1 (RS) Work 6 sc in 2nd ch from hook. Mark last st made with the safety pin. You will be working in a spiral marking the last st made with the safety pin to indicate end of rnd.

Rnd 2 Work 2 sc in each st around—12 sts.

Rnd 3 [Sc in next st, work 2 sc in next st] 6 times—18 sts.

Rnd 4 [Sc in next 2 sts, work 2 sc in next st] 6 times—24 sts.

Rnd 5 [Sc in next 3 sts, work 2 sc in next st] 6 times—30 sts.

Rnd 6–10 Cont to work as established, working 1 more sc between incs every rnd—60 sts.

Rnd 11 Sc in each st around.

Rnd 12 [Sc in next 9 sts, work 2 sc in next st] 6 times—66 sts.

Rnd 13 Rep rnd 11.

Rnd 14 [Sc in next 10 sts, work 2 sc in next st] 6 times—72 sts.

Rnds 15 and 16 Rep rnd 11.

Rnd 17 [Sc in next 11 sts, work 2 sc in next st] 6 times—78 sts.

Rnd 18 Rep rnd 11. Drop safety pin marker. Ch 1, turn.

Divide for front

Row 1 (WS) Sc in next 39 sts. Ch 1, turn.

Row 2 Skip first st, [sc in next 9 sts, work 2 sc in next st] 3 times, sc in each st across, sc in top of t–ch—42 sts. Ch 1, turn.

Rows 3 and 4 Skip first st, sc in each st across, sc in top of t–ch. Ch 1, turn.

Row 5 Skip first st, [sc in next 10 sts, work 2 sc in next st] 3 times, sc in each st across, sc in top of t-ch—45 sts. Ch 1, turn.

Rows 6–21 Rep row 5. Fasten off.

Back

With WS facing, join MC with a sl st in next st after row 1 of front.

Row 1 (WS) Sc in same st as joining, sc in next 39 sts. Ch 1, turn. Beg with row 2, cont to work as for front. Do not fasten off.

Joining front and back

Rnd 1 Sc in each st across back, then front—90 sts. Mark last st made with the safety pin.

Rnds 2–6 Sc in each st around.

Rnd 7 Sl st in each st around. Fasten off.

With A, ch 4.

Rnd 1 (RS) Work 7 dc in 4th ch from hook, join rnd with a sl st in 1st ch of beg ch–4—8 dc (including 3 ch of beg ch–4).

Rnd 2 *Ch 6, insert hook from front to back to front around post of next dc and work a sl st; rep from * around—8 ch–lps. Fasten off. With WS facing, join B with a sl st in any dc of rnd 1.

Rnd 3 (WS) Ch 3 (counts as 1 dc), work 2 dc in same sp as joining, work 3 dc in each dc around, join rnd with a sl st in top of beg ch–3—24 dc. Turn to RS.

Rnd 4 (RS) *Ch 6, skip post of next dc, work sl st around post of next dc; rep from * around—12 ch–lps.

Rnd 5 Work as for rnd 4, working sl sts around skipped posts of rnd 4.

Rnd 6 Sl st in next dc of rnd 3, *ch 6, skip next dc, sl st in next dc; rep from * around. Fasten off.

With C, ch 4.

Row 1 Work 7 dc in 4th ch from hook. Turn.

Row 2 Skip first dc, sl st in next 3 dc, ch 2, work 5 dc in same dc as last sl st. Turn.

Row 3 Skip first dc, sl st in next 2 dc, ch 2, work 5 dc in same dc as last sl st. Turn.

Row 4 Skip first dc, sl st in next 2 dc, ch 2, work 3 dc in same dc as last sl st. Turn.

Row 5 Skip first dc, sl st in next dc, ch 2; in same dc as last sl st, work [yo, insert hook and draw up a lp, yo and draw through 2 lps on hook] twice, yo and draw through all lps on hook. Fasten off.

Felting

Place pieces in a zippered pillowcase and put into washing machine. Use hot-water wash, a regular (not delicate) cycle and the lowest water level. Add a tablespoon of laundry detergent and a pair of old jeans to assist agitation. Agitate twice checking measurements and stopping before spin cycle. Repeat process until tea cozy, when measured flat, measures 12½"/29cm across bottom edge x 9¼"/24cm high (excluding top loop), or size to fit your teapot. Felt flower until it measures 4"/10cm in diameter and leaves 4"/10 long. Gently roll pieces in towels to assist in drying if they are extremely wet. Stretch pieces into shape. Let air dry flat. Use matching thread to sew flower to front of tea cozy, then sew on leaves around flower as pictured.

Jocelyn Sass has created the sweetest lit- tle case to carry your digital camera. It features a bright ribbon carrying strap, a round patch pocket large enough to hold an extra film card and batteries, and a snap closure to prevent your precious cargo from falling out.

FINISHED MEASUREMENTS
■ Approx 5"/12.5cm wide x 5"/12.5cm high (excluding carrying strap)

MATERIALS
■ 1 1.75oz/50g balls (each approx 77yd/ 71m) of Moda Dea/Coats & Clark *Cartwheel* (wool) each in #9745 raspber- ries (MC) and #9748 neapolitan (CC)
■ Size H/8 (5mm) crochet hook *or size to obtain gauge*
■ 11"/28cm length of ⅝"/1.5mm grosgrain ribbon
■ One ½"/1.2cm metal snap set
■ Matching sewing thread
■ Sewing needle

GAUGE
14 sts and 10 rnds to 4"/10cm over hdc using size H/8 (5mm) crochet hook (before felting). *Take time to check gauge.*

HOLDER
With MC, ch 23.

Rnd 1 (RS) Hdc in 3rd ch from hook (first 2 ch count as 1 hdc), hdc in next 19 ch, work 2 hdc in last ch, turn to bottom lps of foundation ch, hdc in next 21 bottom lps, join rnd with a sl st in top of beg ch-2—44 sts. Turn.

Rnds 2–19 Ch 2 (counts as 1 hdc), hdc in each st around, join rnd with a sl st in top of beg ch-2. Turn. When rnd 19 is completed, fasten off.

Pocket
With CC, ch 2.

Rnd 1 (RS) Work 6 sc in 2nd ch from hook, join rnd with a sl st in first sc—6 sts.

Rnd 2 Ch 1, work 2 sc in each st around, join rnd with a sl st in first sc—12 sts.

Rnd 3 Ch 1, *sc in next st, work 2 sc in next st; rep from * around, join rnd with a sl st in first sc—18 sts.

Rnd 4 Ch 1, *sc in next 2 sts, work 2 sc in next st; rep from * around, join rnd with a sl st in first sc—24 sts.

Rnd 5 Ch 1, *sc in next 3 sts, work 2 sc in next st; rep from * around, join rnd with a sl st in first sc—30 sts.

Rnd 6 Ch 1, *sc in next 4 sts, work 2 sc in next st; rep from * around, join rnd with a sl st in first sc—36 sts.

Rnd 7 Ch 1, *sc in next 5 sts, work 2 sc in next st; rep from * around, join rnd with a sl st in first sc—42 sts. Fasten off, leaving a long tail for sewing.

FINISHING
Position pocket on front of holder, placing it between rnds 2–12 and centering it from side to side; pin in place. Using CC, whip-

stitch pocket in place leaving 10 sts across top edge unstitched for pocket opening.

Felting

Place holder in a zippered pillowcase and put into washing machine. Use hot-water wash, a regular (not delicate) cycle and the lowest water level. Add a tablespoon of laundry detergent and an old pair of jeans for agitation. Check piece frequently, agitating until stitches are not seen and holder measures 5"/12.5cm wide x 6"/15cm high. Rinse in cold water, then remove piece from pillowcase. Roll in towels to remove most of the water. Dry in dryer until slightly damp. Hand block to measurements, then stuff lightly with a folded plastic grocery bag to hold its shape. Place on flat surface to air dry. Fold top edge 1"/2.5cm over to RS. Fold one end of ribbon ½"/1.3cm to RS. Position end of ribbon on inside of holder, so folded edge of ribbon is 1"/2.5cm from folded edge and is centered side to side. (RS of ribbon should be facing out.) Sew ribbon end in place using sewing thread. Rep for opposite end of ribbon. On inside front of holder, position top half of snap on top of ribbon end, so edge of snap is ¼"/.6cm from folded edge of ribbon and centered side to side; sew in place. Working in the same manner, sew bottom half of snap to inside back of holder.

Keep your tootsies toasty warm all winter long when you slide into these wooly slippers. Designed by Linda Cyr in basic half-double crochet, they can be made in no time at all.

SIZES

Instructions are written for size Small. Changes for Medium, Large and X-Large are in parentheses.

FINISHED MEASUREMENTS

■ Approx 8½ (9½, 10½, 11½)"/21.5 (24, 26.5, 29) cm long

MATERIALS

■ 3 3.5oz/100g balls (each approx 60yd/ 55m) of Tahki Yarns/Tahki•Stacy Charles, Inc. *Baby* (merino wool) in #14 dark olive (MC)

■ 2 balls in #64 pumpkin (CC)

■ Size K/10½ (6.5mm) crochet hook *or size to obtain gauge*

■ One sheet of extra-stiff quilting template

GAUGE

12 sts to 4"/10cm over dc using size K/10½ (6.5mm) crochet hook (before felting). *Take time to check gauge.*

Note

To join yarn with a sc, make a slip knot and place on hook. Insert hook into st (or lp), yo and draw up a lp, yo and draw through both lps on hook.

INNER SOLE (MAKE 2)

With MC, ch 23 (27, 27, 33).

Rnd I (RS) Work 6 dc in 4th ch from hook, dc in next 18 (22, 22, 28) ch, work 6 dc in last ch, turn to bottom lps of foundation ch, dc in next 18 (22, 22, 28) bottom lps, join rnd with a sl st in 3rd ch of beg.

Rnd 2 Ch 3, dc in same place as joining, *work 2 dc in next 6 sts, dc in next 18 (22, 22, 28) sts; rep from * around once more, join rnd with a sl st in top of beg ch-3.

Rnd 3 Ch 3, dc in same sp as joining, dc in next st, *[work 2 dc in next st, dc in next st] 6 times, dc in next 18 (22, 22, 28) sts; rep from * around once more, join rnd with a sl st in top of beg ch-3.

Rnd 4 Ch 3, dc in same sp as joining, dc in next 2 sts, *[work 2 dc in next st, dc in next 2 sts] 6 times, dc in next 18 (22, 22, 28) sts; rep from * around once more, join rnd with a sl st in top of beg ch-3.

For sizes Small and Medium only
Fasten off.

For sizes Large and X-Large only

Rnd 5 Ch 3, dc in same sp as joining, dc in next 3 sts, *[work 2 dc in next st, dc in next 2 sts] 6 times, dc in next 22 (28) sts; rep from * around once more, join rnd with a sl st in top of beg ch-3. Fasten off.

OUTER SOLE – FOR ALL SIZES (MAKE 2)

With CC, rep as for inner sole.

With MC, ch 25 (25, 29, 29).

Row 1 (RS) Dc in 4th ch from hook, dc in next 9 (9, 11, 11) ch, work 3 dc in next ch, dc in next 11 (11, 13, 13) ch. Ch 3, turn.

Row 2 Skip first 2 sts, dc in next 10 (10, 12, 12) sts, work 3 dc in next st, dc in last 11 (11, 13, 13) sts. Ch 3, turn. Rep row 2 1 (2, 4, 6) times more.

Row 4 (5, 7, 9) Skip first 2 dc, dc in next 22 (22, 26, 26) sts. Ch 3, turn.

Row 5 (6, 8, 10) Skip first 2 sts, dc in next 9 (9, 11, 11) sts, work 3 dc in next st, dc in next 10 (10, 12, 12) sts. Ch 3, turn.

Row 6 (7, 9, 11) Skip first 2 dc, dc in next 20 (20, 24, 24) sts. Ch 3, turn.

Row 7 (8, 10, 12) Skip first 2 sts, dc in next 8 (8, 10, 10) sts, work 3 dc in next st, dc in next 9 (9, 11, 11) sts. Ch 3, turn.

Row 8 (9, 11, 13) Skip first 2 dc, dc in next 18 (18, 22, 22) sts. Fasten off.

Edging

Row 1 (RS) With RS facing, join CC with a sc in first bottom lp of foundation ch, sc in each rem lp across. Fasten off.

Joining top to sole

Center top on toe of MC sole; pin in place.

Rnd 1 (RS) Join CC with a sc in center back heel of sole, sc evenly around entire outer edge, working through both thicknesses to join top and sole where they meet.

Felting

Place slippers in a zippered pillowcase and put into washing machine. Use hot-water wash, a regular (not delicate) cycle and lowest water level. Add a tablespoon of laundry detergent and an old pair of jeans for agitation. Check them every 5–10 minutes, agitating until stitches are not seen and each slipper and sole measures 8½ (9½, 10½, 11½)"/20.5 (24, 26.5, 29)cm long. Rinse in cold water; do not allow to go through spin cycle. Remove from pillowcase, then gently roll in towels to assist in drying if slippers are extremely wet. Hand block to measurements. Let air dry flat for 1 to 2 days. Use unstitched sole to trace outline twice on quilting template for stiffeners. Cut out ⅛"/3mm smaller all around. To finish each slipper, match MC and CC soles and whipstitch edges tog using a double strand of CC, leaving a 3"/7.5cm opening at back heel. Insert stiffener between soles; whipstitch opening closed.

Toss these pillows on your sofa or chair and you'll be tossed plenty of compliments about your crocheting and home decorating skills. The fronts are worked in the round, while the backs are worked back and forth, all in double crochet. Designed by Linda Cyr.

FINISHED MEASUREMENTS
■ Approx 18" x 18"/45.5 x 45.5cm

MATERIALS

Pillow I
■ 5 1.75oz/50g balls (each approx 92yd/84m) of Filatura Di Crosa/Tahki•Stacy Charles, Inc. *127 Print* (wool) in #36 turquoise (A) 🔲
■ 3 balls in #37 pink (B)

Pillow II
■ 7 balls #37 pink (A)
■ 2 balls in #36 turquoise (B)
■ Size I/9 (5.5mm) crochet hook *or size to obtain gauge*
■ Two 16"/40.5 square knife-edge pillow forms

GAUGE

11 sts and 10 rnds to 4"/10cm over dc using size I/9 (5.5mm) crochet hook (before felting). *Take time to check gauge.*

FRONT

Pillow I

Rnd 1 (RS) With A, ch 4 (counts as 1 dc), work 15 dc in 4th ch from hook, join rnd with a sl st in 1st ch of beg ch-4—16 sts.

Rnd 2 Ch 3 (counts as 1 dc), *work (2 dc, ch 1, 2 dc) in next st (corner made), dc in next 3 sts; rep from * around twice more, end work (2 dc, ch 1, 2 dc) in next st, dc in last 2 sts, join rnd with a sl st in top of beg ch-3.

Rnd 3 Sl st in each st to first corner ch-1 sp, ch 3 (counts as 1 dc), work (1 dc, ch 1, 2 dc) in same ch-1 sp, *dc in next 7 sts, work (2 dc, ch 1, 2 dc) in next corner ch-1 sp; rep from * around twice more, end dc in last 7 sts, join rnd with a sl st in top of beg ch-3.

Rnd 4 Sl st in each st to first corner ch-1 sp, ch 3 (counts as 1 dc), work (1 dc, ch 1, 2 dc) in same ch-1 sp, *dc in next 11 sts, work (2 dc, ch 1, 2 dc) in next corner ch-1 sp; rep from * around twice more, end dc in last 11 sts, join rnd with a sl st in top of beg ch-3. Fasten off.

Rnd 5 With RS facing, join B with a sl st in any corner ch-1 sp, ch 3 (counts as 1 dc), work (1 dc, ch 1, 2 dc) in same ch-1 sp, *dc in next 15 sts, work (2 dc, ch 1, 2 dc) in next corner ch-1 sp; rep from * around twice more, end dc in last 15 sts, join rnd with a sl st in top of beg ch-3.

Rnd 6 Sl st in each st to first corner ch-1 sp, ch 3 (counts as 1 dc), work (1 dc, ch 1, 2 dc) in same ch-1 sp, *dc in next 19 sts, work (2 dc, ch 1, 2 dc) in next corner ch-1 sp; rep from * around twice more, end dc in last 19 sts, join rnd with a sl st in top of beg ch-3.

Rnds 7 and 8 Rep rnd 6 working 4 dc more between corner ch-1 sps every rnd. Fasten off.

Rnd 9 With RS facing, join A with a sl st in any corner ch-1 sp, ch 3 (counts as 1 dc), work (1 dc, ch 1, 2 dc) in same ch-1 sp, *dc in next 31 sts, work (2 dc, ch 1, 2 dc) in next corner ch-1 sp; rep from * around twice more, end dc in last 31 sts, join rnd with a sl st in top of beg ch-3.

Rnd 10 Sl st in each st to first corner ch-1 sp, ch 3 (counts as 1 dc), work (1 dc, ch 1, 2 dc) in same ch-1 sp, *dc in next 35 sts, work (2 dc, ch 1, 2 dc) in next corner ch-1 sp; rep from * around twice more, end dc in last 35 sts, join rnd with a sl st in top of beg ch-3.

Rnds 11–13 Rep rnd 10 working 4 dc more between corner ch-1 sps every rnd. Fasten off.

Rnd 14 With RS facing, join B with a sl st in any corner ch-1 sp, ch 3 (counts as 1 dc), work (1 dc, ch 1, 2 dc) in same ch-1 sp, *dc in next 51 sts, work (2 dc, ch 1, 2 dc) in next corner ch-1 sp; rep from * around twice more, end dc in last 51 sts, join rnd with a sl st in top of beg ch-3.

Rnd 15 Sl st in each st to first corner ch-1 sp, ch 3 (counts as 1 dc), work (1 dc, ch 1, 2 dc) in same ch-1 sp, *dc in next 55 sts, work (2 dc, ch 1, 2 dc) in next corner ch-1 sp; rep from * around twice more, end dc in last 55 sts, join rnd with a sl st in top of beg ch-3.

Rnds 16 and 17 Rep rnd 15 working 4 dc more between corner ch-1 sps every rnd. Fasten off.

Pillow II

Work as for pillow I, working rnds 1–4 with A, rnd 5 with B, rnds 6–9 with A, rnd 10 with B, rnds 11–14 with A, rnd 15 with B, and rnds 16 and 17 with A.

Pillow I

With B, ch 71 loosely.

Row 1 (RS) Dc in 4th ch from hook and in each ch across—69 sts. Turn.

Row 2–20 Ch 3 (counts as dc), dc in each st across. Turn. At end of row 20, do not turn. Fasten off.

Pillow II

Work as for pillow I.

With WS facing, pin back pieces to front; back pieces will overlap across center. With RS facing, whipstitch outer edges tog using B; leave back overlap open.

Felting

Place pillow in a zippered pillowcase and put into washing machine. Use hot-water wash, a regular (not delicate) cycle and lowest water level. Add a tablespoon of laundry detergent and an old pair of jeans for agitation. Check every 5–10 minutes, agitating until stitches are not seen and pillow measures 18"/45.5cm square. Rinse in cold water; do not allow to go through spin cycle. Remove from pillowcase, then gently roll in towels to assist in drying if pillow is extremely wet. Hand-block to measurements. Let air dry flat for 1 to 2 days. Insert pillow form.

Fiestable

■■■▢

Linda Medina has come up with a colorful solution to countertop clutter—store it all in a felted tote featuring a fun underwater theme. Crocheted appliqués and French knots give it added dimension.

FINISHED MEASUREMENTS

■ Approx 11¼ "/28.5cm wide (at top) x
7½ "/19cm high x 8¼"/21cm deep (at top)

MATERIALS

■ 5 1.75oz/50g skeins (each approx 93yd/85m) of Nashua Handknits/Westminster Fibers, Inc. *Julia* (wool/alpaca/mohair) in #5185 spring green (MC) (4)

■ 3 skeins in #5178 lupine (A)

■ 1 skein each in #1028 dried wheat (B), #1220 tarnished brass (C), #2250 french pumpkin (D) and #8141 pretty in pink (E)

■ Size G/6 (4mm) crochet hook *or size to obtain gauge*

■ ½yd/.5m lining fabric

■ ⅔yd/.6m ultra-firm, single-side fusible stabilizer

■ Sewing needle and matching sewing threads

GAUGE

15 sts and 18 rows to 4"/10cm over sc using size G/6 (4mm) crochet hook (before felting). *Take time to check gauge.*

Notes

1 When changing colors, draw new color through last 2 lps on hook when working last st.

2 When working French knots, wrap yarn twice around needle.

FRONT

Beg at bottom edge, with MC, ch 53.

Row 1 (RS) Sc in 2nd ch from hook and in each ch across—52 sts. Ch 1, turn.

Rows 2–11 Sc in each st across. Ch 1, turn.

Row 12 Work 2 sc in first sc, sc in each st across to last st, work 2 sc in last sc—54 sts. Ch 1, turn.

Rows 13–22 Rep row 2.

Row 23 Rep row 12—56 sts.

Rows 24 and 25 Rep row 2.

Row 26 Sc in each st across, changing to A. Ch 1, turn.

Rows 27–36 Rep row 2.

Row 37 *Sc in next 2 sts, ch 3, sl st in top of last st made; rep from * across, end sc in last st. Do not cut yarn.

First corner tie

Ch 16.

Row 1 Sc in 2nd ch from hook and in each ch across—15 sts. Join to side edge of row 36 with a sl st. Ch 1, turn.

Row 2 Sc in each st across. Fasten off.

Second corner tie

With RS facing, join MC with a sl st in side edge of row 37. Ch 16. Rep rows 1 and 2 as for first corner tie.

BACK

Work as for front.

SIDE (MAKE 2 PIECES)

Beg at bottom edge, with MC, ch 30.

Row 1 (RS) Sc in 2nd ch from hook and in each ch across—29 sts. Ch 1, turn.

Row 2 Sc in each st across. Ch 1, turn.

Row 3 Work 2 sc in first st, sc in each st to last st, work 2 sc in last st—31 sts. Ch 1, turn.

Rows 4 and 5 Rep row 2.

Row 6 Rep row 3—33 sts.

Rows 7–11 Rep row 2.

Row 12 Rep row 3—35 sts.

Rows 13–17 Rep row 2.

Row 18 Rep row 3—37 sts.

Rows 19–23 Rep row 2.

Row 24 Rep row 3—39 sts.

Row 25 Rep row 2.

Row 26 Sc in each st across, changing to A. Ch 1, turn.

Rows 27–29 Rep row 2.

Row 30 Rep row 3—41 sts.

Rows 31–36 Rep row 2.

Row 37 *Sc in next 2 sts, ch 3, sl st in top of last st made; rep from * across, end sc in last st. Do not cut yarn. First and Second corner ties. Rep rows 1–2 as for first and second corner ties of front.

BOTTOM

With MC, ch 53.

Row 1 (RS) Sc in 2nd ch from hook and in each ch across—52 sts. Ch 1, turn.

Rows 2–33 Sc in each st across. Ch 1, turn. When row 33 is completed, do not ch and turn; fasten off.

LARGE SQUIGGLE (MAKE 12 PIECES)

With D, ch 37.

Row 1 (RS) Sc in 2nd ch from hook, *sc in next ch, skip next 2 ch, sc in next ch, work 3 sc in next ch; rep from * across. Turn.

Row 2 Ch 15, sl st in 2nd ch from hook and in next 13 ch, sl st in last of row 1. Fasten off. Make 5 more using D and 6 using E.

SMALL SQUIGGLE (MAKE 6 PIECES)

With C, ch 27. Rep rows 1 and 2 as for large squiggle.

FINISHING

Felting

Place sides and bottom pieces in a mesh bag. Place large squiggles in a second mesh bag and small squiggles in a third mesh bag. Wash in machine set to hot wash/cold rinse cycle using a small amount of detergent and add several pieces of clothing to agitate. Felt until pieces measure as foll: front and back—10"/25.5cm across bottom edge, 11¼"/28.5cm across top edge and 7½"/19cm high; sides—6"/15cm across bottom edge, 8¼"/21cm across top edge and 7½"/19cm high; bottom—10"/25.5cm x 6"/15cm. Dry in dryer for a few minutes. Pin to measurements. Allow to air dry completely.

Making lining patterns

Draw outline of front, side and bottom onto paper. Add ½"/1.3cm to each side of each outline for seam allowance. Cut out for patterns. Set aside.

Appliqués

Use matching threads. Sew 4 large and 2 small squiggles to both front and back, forming ends into curlicues that face left or right (as shown in photo). Working in the same manner, sew 2 large and 1 small squiggles to side pieces.

Embroidery

Embroider French knots in a random design using colors A to E. Sew front, back and sides to bottom, then sew side seams forming tote.

Lining

Using paper patterns, cut out 2 front pieces, 2 side pieces and 1 bottom piece from lining fabric. Trim off seam allowance from paper patterns. Use patterns to cut out 2 front pieces, 2 side pieces and 1 bottom piece from stabilizer. Fuse stabilizer to back of lining pieces following manufacturer's instructions. Using a ½"/1.3cm seam allowance, baste lining pieces together. Insert lining into tote to check fit, then make any necessary adjustments. Machine–stitch front, back and sides to bottom, then stitch side seams. Insert finished lining into tote. Turn top edge of lining to WS so top edge of lining is ½"/.6cm from top edge; pin. Remove lining; press. Insert lining into tote. Slipstitch top edge of lining in place using sewing thread. At each corner, hold two corner ties together, tightly wrap 6 times with D, then fasten off securely.

■■□□ (colorblock symbols)

To keep baby warm as you stroll with the carriage, try Linda Cyr's lovely pram cover in four pretty shades of wool, and created with lots of pint–size granny squares. Whipstitch squares together before felting.

FINISHED MEASUREMENTS

■ Approx 21½" x 28"/54.5 x 71cm

MATERIALS

■ 1 7oz/200g hank (each approx 364yd/333m) of Naturally NZ/Fiber Trends *Alpine 10–ply* (pure New Zealand wool) each in #2016 gray (A), #2014 pink (B), #2002 lime (C) and #2009 seafoam (D) (4)

■ Size N/15 (10mm) crochet hook *or size to obtain gauge*

GAUGE

One square to 4¼"/11cm using size N/15 (10mm) crochet hook with 2 strands of yarn held tog (before felting).

Take time to check gauge.

Note

Use 2 strands of yarn held tog throughout.

SQUARE (MAKE 63)

With 2 strands of A, held tog, ch 4. Join ch with a sl st forming a ring.

Rnd 1 (RS) Ch 3 (counts as 1 dc), work 2 dc in ring, [ch 3, work 3 dc in ring] 3 times, ch 3, join rnd with a sl st in top of beg ch-3.

Rnd 2 Ch 4 (counts as 1 dc and ch 1), [work (3 dc, ch 3, 3 dc) in next ch-3 sp, ch 1] 3 times, work (3 dc, ch 3, 2 dc) in last ch-3 sp, join rnd with a sl st in 3rd ch of beg ch-4. Fasten off. Make 15 squares more using A, 16 each using B and C, and 15 using D.

FINISHING

Using A and working in back lps, whipstitch squares tog foll placement diagram.

Edging

With RS facing, join 2 strands of B with a sl st in any corner ch-3 sp.

Rnd 1 (RS) Ch 1, work 3 sc in same sp as joining, sc in each st around, working 3 sc in each ch-3 corner sp, join rnd with a sl st in first sc. Fasten off.

Felting

Place lap robe in a zippered pillowcase and put into washing machine. Use hot-water wash, a regular (not delicate) cycle and lowest water level. Add a tablespoon of laundry detergent and an old pair of jeans for agitation. Check piece every 5–10 minutes, agitating until stitches are not seen and piece measures 21½" x 28"/54.5 x 71cm. Rinse in cold water; do not allow to go through spin cycle. Remove from pillowcase, then gently roll in towels to assist in drying if lap robe is extremely wet. Hand-block to measurements. Let air dry flat for 1 to 2 days.

A	D	C	B	A	D	C
B	A	D	C	B	A	D
C	B	A	D	C	B	A
D	C	B	A	D	C	B
A	D	C	B	A	D	C
B	A	D	C	B	A	D
C	B	A	D	C	B	A
D	C	B	A	D	C	B
C	B	A	D	C	B	A

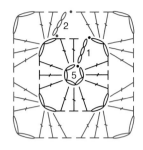

Stitch Key

⌒ Chain

• Slip Stitch

╤ Double Crochet

Red rover

This fabulous shoulder tote is sure to become a wardrobe staple. Designed by Linda Cyr in hot red with ebony-black trim, the size is just right and it will always be in fashion. The felting process not only creates a durable fabric but also gives an air of sophistication to the humble single crochet stitch.

■ Approx 10"/25.5cm wide x 10"/25.5 high x 3½"/9cm deep (excluding straps)

MATERIALS

■ 3 3.5oz/100g balls (each approx 210yd/192m) of Plymouth Yarn Co. *Galway Worsted* (wool) in #16 red (MC) **④**
■ 1 ball in #9 black (CC)
■ Size J/10 (6mm) crochet hook *or size to obtain gauge*
■ One 1"/25mm button
■ Small safety pin

GAUGE

11 sts to 4"/10cm over sc using size J/10 (6mm) crochet hook (before felting).
Take time to check gauge.

SHOULDER BAG

Bottom

With MC, ch 45.

Row 1 Sc in 2nd ch from hook and in each ch across—44 sts. Ch 1, turn.

Rows 2–16 Sc in each sc across. Ch 1, turn.

When row 16 is completed, ch 1, turn to short edge.

Sides

Rnd 1 Work 1 sc in each of next 16 rows, turn to bottom lps of beg ch; sc in next 44 bottom lps, turn to next short edge; work 1 sc in each of next 16 rows, turn to top edge; sc in last 44 sts—120 sts. Mark last st made with the safety pin. You will be working in a spiral marking the last st made with the safety pin to indicate end of rnd.

Rnds 2–54 Sc in each st around. When rnd 54 is completed, join rnd with a sl st in first st changing to CC. Drop safety pin.

Rnd 55 Ch 1, sc in each sc around, join rnd with a sl st in first st.

Rnd 56 Sl st in each sc around. Mark last st made with the safety pin.

Rnds 57 and 58 Sl st in each sc of rnd 55. When rnd 58 is completed, fasten off.

CLOSING TAB

With MC, ch 14.

Row 1 (RS) Sc in 2nd ch from hook and in each ch across—13 sts. Ch 1, turn.

Rows 2–24 Sc in each sc across, Ch 1, turn.

Row 25 (buttonhole) Skip first sc, sc in next 3 sts, ch 4, skip next 4 sts, sc in next 3 sts, skip next st, sc in last st—7 sc and 4 ch. Ch 1, turn.

Row 26 Skip first sc, sc in next 3 sts, sc in next 4 ch, sc in last 3 sts—10 sts. Ch 1, turn.

Row 27 Skip first st, sc in next 7 sts, skip next st, sc in last st—8 sts. Ch 1, turn.

Row 28 Skip first st, sc in next 5 sts, skip next st, sc in last st—6 sts. Fasten off.

Edging

With RS facing, join CC with a sl st in side edge of row 1.

Row 1 (RS) Sc in each st and row around to opposite side of row 1. Turn.

Row 2 Sl st in each st across. Turn.

Row 3 Sl st in each sc of row 1. Fasten off.

Circles (make 2)

With MC, ch 4.

Rnd 1 (RS) Work 11 dc in 4th ch from hook, join rnd with a sl st in 1st ch of beg ch-4—12 dc (including 3 ch of beg ch-4). Fasten off. Set circles aside.

First half of strap and first circle

With CC, ch 100.

Rnd 1 With RS of first circle facing, work 2 sc in each dc around—24 sts. Mark last st made with the safety pin.

Rnd 2 Sl st in each sc around.

Second half of strap and second circle

Turn to bottom lps of chain, dc in each bottom lp across.

Rnd 1 With RS of second circle facing, work 2 sc in each dc around—24 sts. Mark last st made with the safety pin.

Rnd 2 Sl st in each sc around. Join rnd with a sl st in side edge of strap. Fasten off.

Position and pin straight edge of closing tab to inside back of bag, so straight edge of tab is 1½"/4cm from top edge of bag and is centered side to side. Whipstitch edge in place using MC. Position and pin strap circles to front of bag, so bottom edge of circles are 4"/10cm from top edge of bag and outside edges are 2½"/6.5cm from side edges of bag. Sew MC section of circles in place using MC. Working in the same manner, sew rem strap to back of bag.

Felting

Place bag in a zippered pillowcase and put into washing machine. Use hot-water wash, a regular (not delicate) cycle and lowest water level. Add a tablespoon of laundry detergent and an old pair of jeans for agitation. Check piece every 5–10 minutes, agitating until stitches are not seen and bag measures 10"/25.5cm wide x 10"/25.5 high x 3½"/9cm deep. Rinse in cold water; do not allow to go through spin cycle. Remove from pillowcase, then gently roll in towels to assist in drying if bag is extremely wet. Hand block to measurements. Place bag on a flat surface. Arrange straps so they are smooth and straight. Let air dry flat for 1 to 2 days. Sew button between front circles.

BUTTERFLY TOY

Fuzzy flyer

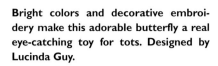

Bright colors and decorative embroidery make this adorable butterfly a real eye-catching toy for tots. Designed by Lucinda Guy.

■ Approx 6½"/16.5cm wide x 6¼"/16cm high (including antennae)

MATERIALS

■ 1 1.75oz/50g ball (each approx 109yd/99m) of Reynolds/JCA Inc. *Lite-Lopi* (Icelandic wool) each in #441 leaf (MC), #435 goldenrod (A) and #436 pumpkin (B)

■ Size H/8 (5mm) crochet hook *or size to obtain gauge*
■ Polyester fiberfill
■ Small safety pin

GAUGE

16 sts and 17 rows to 4"/10cm over sc using size H/8 (5mm) crochet hook (before felting). *Take time to check gauge.*

Notes

1 To join yarn with a sc, make a slip knot and place on hook. Insert hook into st, yo and draw up a lp, yo and draw through both lps on hook.

2 When changing colors, draw new color through last 2 lps on hook to complete last st.

3 When working French knots, wrap yarn 4 times around needle.

STITCH GLOSSARY

sc2tog [Insert hook in next st, yo and draw up a lp] twice, yo and draw through all 3 lps on hook.

BODY

With MC, ch 8.

Row 1 (RS) Sc in 2nd ch from hook and in each ch across—7 sts. Turn.

Rows 2 and 3 Ch 1, sc in each st across. Turn.

Row 4 Ch 1, 2 sc in first st, sc in each st to last st, work 2 sc in last st—9 sts. Turn.

Rows 5 and 6 Rep row 2.

Row 7 Rep row 4—11 sts.

Rows 8–15 Rep row 2.

Row 16 Ch 1, sc2tog, sc in each st to last 2 sts, sc2tog—9 sts. Turn.

Row 17 Rep row 2.

Row 18 Rep row 16—7 sts.

Rows 19 and 20 Rep row 2. Fasten off. Turn.

Right antennae

Row 1 (RS) With RS facing, skip first 2 sts of row 20, join MC with a sc in next st, sc in same st, leaving rem 4 sts unworked—2 sts. Turn.

Rows 2–6 Ch 1, sc in each st across. Fasten off leaving a long tail for sewing. Turn.

Row 7 With RS facing, join A with a sc in first st, work 2 more sc in same st, work 3 sc in next st—6 sts. Turn.

Row 8 Ch 1, sc in each st across. Fasten off leaving a long tail for sewing.

Left antennae

Row 1 (RS) With RS facing, skip center st of row 20, join MC with a sc in next st, sc in same st, leaving rem 2 sts unworked—2 sts. Turn. Cont to work as for right antennae.

LARGE WINGS (MAKE 4 PIECES)

With MC, ch 4. Join ch with a sl st forming a ring.

Rnd 1 (RS) Work 8 sc in ring, changing to A. Mark last st made with the safety pin. You will be working in a spiral marking the last st made with the safety pin to indicate end of rnd.

Rnd 2 With A, work 2 sc in each st around, changing to MC—16 sts.

Rnd 3 With MC, [work 2 sc in next st, sc in next st] 8 times, changing to A—24 sts.

Rnd 4 With A, [work 2 sc in next st, sc in next 2 sts] 8 times—32 sts.

Rnd 5 [Work 2 sc in next st, sc in next 3 sts] 8 times—40 sts. Fasten off.

SMALL WINGS (MAKE 4 PIECES)

Work rnds 1–3 as for large wings.

FINISHING

For each antenna, use MC tail to whipstitch seam of MC section. Use A tail to whipstitch seam of A section, then sew running stitches around between rows 6 and 7. Pull yarn to gather in; fasten off securely.

Embroidery

For body, count 4 rows from the bottom.

With A, *work a cross–stitch over center 3 sts and 1 row, skip 1 row; rep from * 3 times more. With B, sew a vertical straight stitch over center of each cross stitch. For large wings, use B to embroider 15 French knots spaced evenly around, between rnds 4 and 5. For small wings, use B to embroider 6 French knots spaced evenly around, between rnds 2 and 3.

Felting

Place pieces in a zippered pillowcase and put into washing machine. Use hot-water wash, a regular (not delicate) cycle and the lowest water level. Add a tablespoon of laundry detergent and an old pair of jeans for agitation. Check pieces frequently, agitating until body measures 3¾"/9.5cm wide x 4¾"/126cm high (excluding antennae), large wings 2⅞"/cm in diameter and small wings 2"/5cm in diameter. Rinse in cold water, then remove pieces from pillowcase. Roll pieces in towels to remove most of the water. Place pieces in a dry zippered pillowcase, then dry in dryer until they are slightly damp. Hand block each piece to measurements. Let air dry on a flat surface. Sew pieces as foll: beg at top edge of body, use MC to whipstitch seam leaving bottom edge open. Stuff body firmly with fiberfill. Sew running stitches around bottom edge of body. Pull yarn to gather in and close opening; fasten off securely. With A, whip stitch two pairs of large wings tog. With MC, whipstitch two pairs of small wings tog. Pin large wings to sides of body, positioning each between rows 13 and 16. Whipstitch in place using MC. Position, then pin, each small wing so it touches body and large wing. Whipstitch in place using MC.

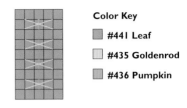

Color Key

■ #441 Leaf

□ #435 Goldenrod

■ #436 Pumpkin

■■■◻

Mineral colors and graphic Andean-inspired designs make this crocheted-in-the-round tote a gem. You'll have the best of both worlds, because it's rugged enough for hiking through the country-side, yet right in fashion for strolling around the city. Designed by Marty Miller.

FINISHED MEASUREMENTS
■ Approx 8½ "/21.5cm diameter x 11"/ 28cm length (excluding straps)

MATERIALS
■ 2 3.5oz/100g skeins (each approx 220yd/201m) of Cascade Yarns *Cascade 220* (wool) each in #9420 teal (A) and #8885 plum (C) (④)
■ 1 skein in #7823 goldenrod (B)
■ Size L/11 (8mm) crochet hook *or size to obtain gauge*
■ Safety pins

GAUGE
10 sts and 12 rnds to 4"/10cm over sc using size L/11 (8mm) crochet hook (before felting). *Take time to check gauge.*

Notes
1 When changing colors on rnds, draw new color through when joining.
2 When changing colors on rows, draw new color through last 2 lps on hook when working last st.
3 When working chart pats, carry color not in use loosely on WS of work. On next rnd,

work over the loose strands.
4 When working stripes on rnds, carry colors up loosely on WS of work.

BAG
With A, ch 2.
Rnd 1(RS) Work 6 sc in 2nd ch from hook, join rnd with a sl st in first st.
Rnd 2 Ch 1, work 2 sc in each st around, join rnd with a sl st in first st changing to B—12 sts.
Rnd 3 Ch 1, *work 2 sc in next st, sc in next st; rep from * around, join rnd with a sl st in first st—18 sts.
Rnd 4 Ch 1, *work 2 sc in next st, sc in next 2 sts; rep from * around, join rnd with a sl st in first st changing to C—24 sts.
Rnd 5 Ch 1, *work 2 sc in next st, sc in next 3 sts; rep from * around, join rnd with a sl st in first st—30 sts.
Rnd 6 Ch 1, *work 2 sc in next st, sc in next 4 sts; rep from * around, join rnd with a sl st in first st changing to A—36 sts.
Rnd 7 Ch 1, *work 2 sc in next st, sc in next 5 sts; rep from * around, join rnd with a sl st in first st—42 sts.
Rnd 8 Ch 1, *work 2 sc in next st, sc in next 6 sts; rep from * around, join rnd with a sl st in first st changing to B—48 sts.
Rnd 9 Ch 1, *work 2 sc in next st, sc in next 7 sts; rep from * around, join rnd with a sl st in first st—54 sts.
Rnd 10 Ch 1, *work 2 sc in next st, sc in next 8 sts; rep from * around, join rnd with

a sl st in first st changing to C—60 sts.

Rnd 11 Ch 1, *work 2 sc in next st, sc in next 9 sts; rep from * around, join rnd with a sl st in first st—66 sts.

Rnd 12 Ch 1, *work 2 sc in next st, sc in next 10 sts; rep from * around, join rnd with a sl st in first st changing to A—72 sts.

Rnd 13 Ch 1, *work 2 sc in next st, sc in next 11 sts; rep from * around, join rnd with a sl st in first st—78 sts.

Rnd 14 Ch 1, *work 2 sc in next st, sc in next 12 sts; rep from * around, join rnd with a sl st in first st changing to B—84 sts.

Rnd 15 Ch 1, *work 2 sc in next st, sc in next 13 sts; rep from * around, join rnd with a sl st in first st—90 sts.

Rnd 16 Ch 1, *work 2 sc in next st, sc in next 14 sts; rep from * around, join rnd with a sl st in first st changing to C—96 sts.

Rnd 17 Ch 1, *work 2 sc in next st, sc in next 15 sts; rep from * around, join rnd with a sl st in first st—102 sts.

Rnd 18 Ch 1, *work 2 sc in next st, sc in next 16 sts; rep from * around, join rnd with a sl st in first st changing to A—108 sts.

Rnds 19 and 20 Ch 1, sc in each st around, join rnd with a sl st in first st.

Beg chart pat

Rnd 1 (RS) Ch 1, beg with st 1 and work to st 12, work 12–st rep 8 times more, join rnd with a sl st in first st. Cont to foll chart in this way to rnd 44, changing colors as needed. Fasten off.

STRAPS (MAKE 2)

Center section

With A, ch 61.

Row 1 (RS) Sc in 2nd ch from hook and each ch across, changing to B. Ch 1, turn.

Row 2 Sc in each st across. Ch 1, turn.

Row 3 Sc in each st across, changing to C. Ch 1, turn.

Rows 4, 6, 8, 10 Rep row 2.

Row 5 Sc in each st across, changing to A. Ch 1, turn.

Row 7 Sc in each st across, changing to B. Ch 1, turn.

Row 9 Sc in each st across, changing to C. Ch 1, turn.

Row 11 Sc in each st across, changing to A. Ch 1, turn.

Row 12 Sc in each sc across. Ch 1, turn.

Joining

With RS facing, fold center section in half, bringing bottom lps of foundation ch up to row 12.

Next row (RS) Insert hook in first st of row 12 and into first bottom lp of foundation ch, yo, draw up a lp, yo and draw through 2 lps on hook (sc st and bottom lp tog), *sc in next st and next bottom lp tog; rep from * across. Fasten off.

End section

Row 1 (RS) With RS of center section facing, join A with a sc in side edge of first row, then sc in side edge of next 11 rows—12 sts. Turn.

Rows 2–19 Ch 1, sc in each st across. Turn.
Row 20 Ch 1, sc in each st across. Fasten off. Rep rows 1–20 at opposite end of center section.

With RS of top edge facing, use safety pins to mark sts as foll: 1, 12, 28, 39, 55, 66, 82, 93. With RS tog and A, sc end section of a strap to top of tote between sts 1 and 12, then opposite end of same strap between sts 28 and 29. With RS tog and A, sc end section of rem strap between sts 55 and 66, then opposite end of same strap between sts 82 and 93.

Felting

Place tote in a zippered pillowcase. Set the water level on your washing machine to low, and the temperature to hot. Put in a little clear laundry detergent, an old towel or two (or a pair of old jeans, or a couple of rubber balls or flip flops) to help with agitation. Set your washer for a heavy load and check the felting progress every 5 or 10 minutes. Do not let the tote go through the spin cycle, as this may cause creasing. You may have to repeat this felting process one or more times to adequately felt the tote and until it measures 8½"/21.5cm wide x 11"/28cm. If so, drain the water from the washing machine each time and start again. You may also add some boiling water to the machine. When the tote is felted, rinse it in cold water, and roll it in a towel to squeeze out the excess water. Hand block to measurements. Place tote on a flat surface. Stuff with newspaper to wick away the water and help it dry. Arrange straps so they are smooth and straight. Let air dry flat for 1 to 2 days.

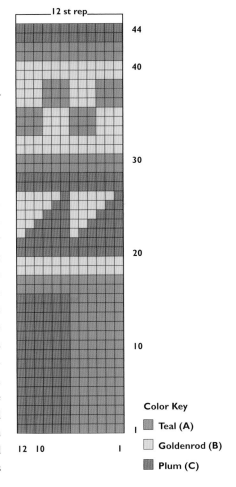

Color Key
Teal (A)
Goldenrod (B)
Plum (C)

RESOURCES

*Write to the yarn
companies listed below for
purchasing and mail-order
information.*

Berroco, Inc.
P.O. Box 367
14 Elmdale Road
Uxbridge, MA 01569
www.berroco.com

Brown Sheep Company
100662 County Road 16
Mitchell, NE 69357
www.brownsheep.com

Cascade Yarns
1224 Andover Park East
Tukwila, WA 98188
www.cascadeyarns.com

Classic Elite Yarns
122 Western Avenue
Lowell, MA 01851
www.classiceliteyarns.com

Coats & Clark
3430 Toringdon Way
Suite 301
Charlotte, NC 28277
www.coatsandclark.com

Crystal Palace Yarns
160 23rd Street
Richmond, CA 94804
www.crystalpalaceyarns.com

Fiber Trends
P.O. Box 7266
E. Wenatchee, WA 98802
www.fibertrends.com

Filatura Di Crosa
distributed by
Tahki•Stacy Charles, Inc.

JCA, Inc.
35 Scales Lane
Townsend, MA 01469
www.jcacrafts.com

KFI
P.O. Box 336
315 Bayview Avenue
Amityville, New York 11701
www.knittingfever.com

Lion Brand Yarn
34 West 15th Street
New York, NY 10011
www.lionbrand.com

Lorna's Laces
4229 North Honore Street
Chicago, IL 60613
www.lornaslaces.net

Louet North America
808 Commerce Park Drive
Ogdensburg, NY 13669

Moda Dea
distributed by
Coats & Clark
www.modadea.com

Nashua Handknits
distributed by
Westminster Fibers, Inc.

Naturally NZ
15 Church Street
Onehunga
Auckland, New Zealand
www.naturallyyarnsnz.com

In the US:
distributed by
Fiber Trends

Noro
distributed by
KFI

Plymouth Yarn Co.
P.O. Box 28
Bristol, PA 19007
www.plymouthyarn.com

Reynolds
distributed by
JCA, Inc.

Tahki•Stacy Charles, Inc.
70-30 80th Street
Building #36
Ridgewood, NY 11385
www.tahkistacycharles.com

Tahki Yarns
distributed by
Tahki•Stacy Charles, Inc.

Westminster Fibers
165 Ledge Street
Nashua, NH 03060
www.westminsterfibers.com

CANADIAN RESOURCES

Write to U.S. resources for mail-order availability of yarns not listed.

Louet North America
R.R. 4
Prescott, Ontario
Canada K0E 1T0
www.louet.com

Naturally NZ
distributed by
The Old Mill Knitting
Company

Patons
320 Livingstone Avenue
 South
Listowel, Ontario
Canada N4W 3H3
www.patonsyarns.com

**The Old Mill Knitting
Company**
P.O. Box 81176
Ancaster, Ontario
Canada L9G 4X2
www.oldmillknitting.com

FELTED CROCHET ON THE GO!

Editorial Director
ELAINE SILVERSTEIN

Book Division Manager
ERICA SMITH

Executive Editor
CARLA SCOTT

Art Director
DIANE LAMPHRON

Associate Art Director
SHEENA PAUL

Yarn Editor
TANIS GRAY

Instructions Editors
PAT HARSTE
JEANNIE CHIN

Photography
JACK DEUTSCH STUDIO

Copy Editor
KRISTINA SIGLER

■

Vice President, Publisher
TRISHA MALCOLM

Production Manager
DAVID JOINNIDES

Creative Director
JOE VIOR

President
ART JOINNIDES